How to Make Your Realtor® Get You the Best Deal

Kathie Moore –

For providing criticism that's easy to take.

To your success.

Ken DesRoches

How to Make Your Realtor® Get You the Best Deal

Step-by-Step Instructions for Selecting and Working With a Realtor® So That Your Home Purchase Can Be the Best Deal Ever!

by
Ken Deshaies

Gabriel Publications

Published by:
Gabriel Publications
14340 Addison St. #101
Sherman Oaks, California 91423
(818) 906-2147 Voice
(818) 990-8631 Fax
www.InstantAuthor.com

Distributed by:
Gabriel Publications
Typography: Synergistic Data Systems, sdsdesign@earthlink.net
Cover Design: Dale Schroeder, SDS

Manufactured in the United States of America

Contents

Part One:
The Home Buying Process, A Brief History

Part Two:
A New Law for the People

Part Three:
Let's Get Started

Part Four:
Getting Your Home

Appendices

Acknowledgments

There are those without whom I would not have written this book. They deserve more than the recognition given here. Their faith in me, at times, exceeded my own.

Sloan Bashinski, who in 1984, published a book called *Home Buyers: Lambs to the Slaughter?*, which has served as an inspiration to me in my real estate practice.

My friend and teacher, **J. Albert Bauer**, who is the attorney for the Summit Association of Realtors®, a member of the Approved Forms Committee for the Colorado Real Estate Commission, and a trainer of Realtors®. "Jay" was kind enough to edit the book with an eye to legal and technical issues. His contributions were invaluable.

My wife and business partner, **Mary**, who helped with typing. In addition to carving time out of her hectic schedule, she made me find the time I claimed I didn't have.

My sister-in-law, **Anna Warner**, who became the first reader of the book, and edited brilliantly, with insight and sensitivity.

My publisher, **Rennie Gabriel**, who constantly prodded without pushing, and who was a constant source of inspiration and ideas.

The **hundreds of clients** with whom Mary and I have worked through the years who have provided the fodder for this book.

Patricia McDade, founder and inspirational leader of The Entrepreneurial Edge, who is dragging me kicking and screaming into an understanding and a practice that, in this world, anything is possible.

And my business coach, **Bill Rogers**, who has always inspired me to do more with my life than I ever thought possible, and who provided the following quote, which serves as a screen saver on my computer:

"You don't end up in the grave. You end up in the hearts of the people you have touched."

—Ken Deshaies

Disclaimer

I've tried. Believe me, I have attempted to ensure that everything said here is accurate and relevant. But laws change, circumstances vary, and there is always the possibility for error. Using the guidance that is offered here, along with your selection of a competent real estate professional, you should feel confident in purchasing a residence. If your purchase is complicated by any of a myriad of factors (e.g., it's a business, it's a farm or ranch, it has well, septic, soil or title problems), I recommend you consult with a Realtor® who specializes in that area or your attorney or other professionals who can assist with the specifics involved.

About gender usage: in order to avoid numerous grammatical messes and to make the reading flow better, I have used "he" and "him" instead of "he or she" or "him or her" throughout this book. So please understand that the use of the male pronoun includes the female usage as well.

About use of the term *Realtor®*: the term *Realtor®* is a trademark of the National Association of Realtors®, and anyone who uses that term as part of his professional identity must be a member, not only of the National Association of Realtors® (NAR), but also of his local and state associations. Please see Chapter 7 for a more complete explanation.

Preface

When Sloan Bashinski wrote his groundbreaking book, *Home Buyers: Lambs to the Slaughter?* in 1984, the rules and laws were vastly different than they are today. Through my publisher, I had originally consulted with Sloan about updating his book, but found the differences too daunting, and a transition too confusing. Besides, I felt that you, the reader, care more about how to navigate in today's world, and in this context probably have only a passing interest in what went on in the past. Therefore, this book is dedicated to you and attempts to provide you with the tools to make the process work for you.

In the hundreds of cases in which I have represented buyers, and in observing hundreds of other transactions where other Realtors® were involved, I have found one overriding factor which can make the difference between a successful home purchase and one that is less than satisfactory.

The difference is **Service.** The level of service provided by your Realtor®, and the attitude he carries into the transaction, will translate either into knowledgeable and fully informed consumers at the closing table or into frustration, ill feelings, and even last-minute surprises. No one wants to be surprised where money is concerned, especially when it's costing you more than you thought. I've found even that a certain degree of incompetence can be overcome by a real estate professional who tries harder, is not afraid to ask lots of questions, and keeps your best interests in mind before his or her commission.

This book is clearly biased, as all books are that advocate a position. It represents my view of the world. Though it is a view I feel is valid, other views exist, some very contradictory to mine. Nevertheless, I believe this book will show you how to get the most service from your Realtor® and how to ensure that key person is on your side. I hope you find it valuable.

About the Author

KEN DESHAIES is a Realtor® in Colorado. A broker who is also an Accredited Buyer Representative (ABR) and Graduate from the Realtor® Institute (GRI), he began his real estate career in Denver in 1992, and since 1994, has worked in Summit County. He is affiliated with RE/MAX Properties of the Summit and works in partnership with his wife, Mary. Located an hour west of Denver, Summit County is home to four ski resorts and the highest freshwater sailing lake in the United States. Since he moved to the mountains, he has happily not worn a tie. For several years, Ken served as the chairperson of the Professional Standards Committee of the Summit Association of Realtors®, the committee that oversees the ethical conduct of Association members. This book is based primarily on his experience working with buyers. Purchasing resort real estate, while similar in many ways to buying in a metropolitan area, offers unique problems for locals and first-time home-buyers as well as for out-of-area investors.

Prior to real estate, Ken owned a private investigations firm for 12 years in Denver, employing and supervising as many as seven investigators and serving for a period as the President of the Professional Private Investigators Association of Colorado. In this work, he conducted numerous investigations into real estate transactions and claims of fraud. During much of this time, he was also a member of the Win/Win Business Forum of Denver and was its president for a year and a half.

To Reach Ken Deshaies
ken@snowhome.com
or see page 101

Introduction

What Could Possibly Go Wrong?

Life would be great if we didn't have to practice diligence in nearly every action we take. From setting up your bedside alarm clock, to purchasing stereos and appliances, to buying a home, we have a primary responsibility to be aware of the potential pitfalls. Unfortunately, most people pay less attention to the process of buying their home than they do when buying a television set. Admittedly, because the process is much more complicated and requires more knowledge, the vast majority of home-buyers work with a professional. However, this doesn't necessarily remove the obstacles or protect us from financial or physical injury. Your home purchase will likely be the most important transaction of your lifetime. The results of that decision are generally long-term, good or bad. The following examples are situations that have gone bad, even though a professional was involved. The rest of this book is designed to help you make that transaction a positive one with long-term benefits.

Roof Leaks Don't Lie

Some years ago, when I was still a private investigator, I received a call from an attorney who represented the Gordons, a couple who had recently bought a great old Hilltop home. Hilltop has always been a popular "moving up" area of Denver and is known for a certain degree of wealth and status, though the residences there are not ostentatious.

It seems the Gordons, in the moving-in process, filled the garage with dozens of boxes, many of which contained an old and rare book collection they had been adding to for many years. The first weekend after they had moved in, before they finished unpacking, there was a rainstorm. Colorado is known for its summer "gully washers," rain storms that may last for only half an hour to an hour, but dump tremendous amounts of rain and literally "wash out" the gullies, curbs and drainage systems. This was a true gully washer.

The Gordons never anticipated what would happen during that storm. It rained inside the garage, destroying a significant amount of their rare book collection along with lots of other household items. Of course, the Gordons were away at the time, so the situation progressed unimpeded. The Gordons were devastated when they returned home.

They had, of course, had a professional home inspection when they were under contract to purchase the home, and the inspector did not indicate the presence of any roof leaks. They contacted their Realtor®, who had recommended the home inspector, and asked for assistance. She contacted the sellers' Realtor®, who professed no knowledge, then purportedly contacted the sellers, who also claimed innocence. The Gordons, in their extreme frustration, hired an attorney, who contacted me to conduct a thorough investigation.

The resulting lawsuit named several people—the sellers, the sellers' Realtor®, the home inspector, the buyers' Realtor®, and the two brokers—and here is why each was culpable.

The Sellers

My investigation revealed that the sellers had experienced roof leaks as a matter of course for several years. It was a Spanish style tile roof and very expensive to repair or replace. I had located the roofing company that had performed repairs to the roof through the years. I obtained a statement from the owner of the company that, two years prior to the sale, he had told the sellers that he refused to do any more repairs to the roof, because the patchwork was not working. The roof needed to be replaced. That disclosure to the sellers was also in writing from the roofing company. The Sellers' Property Disclosure, given to the buyers during the contract period, indicated that the roof was sound and had no leaks.

The Sellers' Realtor®

The Sellers' Realtor® was well-known. She had been in business for many years and had a reputation for specializing in high-end listings in the Cherry Creek, Hilltop, Mayfair and surrounding subdivisions in east Denver. She was also known for "dressing up" her listings so that they would sell quicker. That is, she would instruct her sellers to paint and do other cosmetic work to make the house look its best, and she would even lend expensive furniture when it would help make the home look luxurious. When I met with her and her broker, she denied any knowledge of roof leaks or other problems pertaining to the house. I was able to determine that she had instructed the sellers to paint parts of the interior of the home. I later learned from other sources that she had specifically noticed water stains on living room, dining room and other walls, and had ordered those walls painted so that the water stains would not be noticed by visiting prospective buyers.

3

The Home Inspector

Before meeting with the original home inspector, I hired another, and we had gone through the home in some detail. Among other things, we noted that in the attic, the sellers had placed sheets of plastic, each of which showed dried water marks. It was clear that the sheets of plastic were meant to capture water leaking from the roof. When I interviewed the home inspector, he admitted that he had never gone into the attic (even to inspect the insulation). He also admitted that he had no money and no insurance and didn't even own a home; he said, "So sue me. I'll just go out of business." In fact, he was not bonded or insured, and didn't even have any formal training (such as certification through the American Society of Home Inspectors or similar organization).

The Buyers' Realtor®

Of all the parties, this lady was the most innocent. She truly felt she had done her job and was straightforward in her interview with me. She was also fairly new in the business, with a little more than a year of experience at the time she worked with the Gordons. However, she had made a serious mistake. She had recommended a home inspector, without having checked out his credentials or reputation, and without even verifying that he was bonded and/or insured. The simple action of checking with her broker or other agents in her office to make sure her buyers had a truly professional inspector would have prevented this entire incident, in spite of the efforts on the parts of the sellers and their Realtor® to hide the evidence.

The Brokers

Regardless of the direct liability and culpability of the agents involved, they work for, and under the supervision of, their brokers. In both cases, the brokers either failed to train their agents properly or failed to supervise their actions effectively. Hence, they were named in the lawsuit.

The Result

The Gordons won their lawsuit. However, it took more than a year, and in the meantime, they had to finance a complete roof replacement on their own. It was also difficult to accurately ascertain the value of the rare books they lost, so the amount they collected for lost goods was far less than what they felt they should have gotten. And, of course, they received no compensation for the psychological pain and suffering they endured, nor for the time lost from work pursuing the lawsuit. So, in spite of the fact that some justice was eventually served, no one came out a true winner. And the entire mess could have been avoided with good representation and a little dose of honesty.

The Telltale Garbage

A few years ago, my friends the Crandalls, were moving back to Colorado and told me they were looking for a home in another town. Since I didn't sell real estate in that area, I offered to refer them to a Realtor® who would represent their best interests. However, they said they had already gotten a referral from another friend and had met with that Realtor®, whom I'll call Jeremy. So, I simply recommended ways they could check out the history and reputation of Jeremy and suggested they insist that Jeremy enter into a buyer-agency contract with them. Then they would be legally represented, especially important since they would be engaging in a home purchase at a long distance from their current home on the East Coast.

But you know how it is. You can give people advice with good intentions, but then it's up to them to take it. People don't like to have advice forced on them. A few months later, sometime after the sale, I next talked with the Crandalls. They had moved into their new home and had invited us to dinner. They spent most of the evening complaining about the problems they had been forced to endure in the real estate transaction.

It appears that their Realtor® was virtually non-existent from the time they went under contract until closing. It also turns out he had sold the Crandalls his own listing, and represented the seller in the transaction. He had refused to enter into a contract to represent the buyers because it was "against my company's policy," and the Crandalls did not press the issue. Jeremy did recommend a home inspector, and on one of her trips to Colorado, Alice Crandall met with the inspector to go through the house. Jeremy did not attend the inspection. There were a number of items that needed to be repaired, including a failing heating system, and after returning home, Alice wrote Jeremy asking him to request the sellers make the repairs.

The response from the sellers was that a number of the items would be taken care of prior to closing, and the Crandalls left the responsibility of overseeing those items to their "trusted" Realtor®.

The Crandalls then arrived in Colorado on the day of the closing. Before arriving at the closing, however, they drove by the house. In the driveway, directly in front of the garage, there was a huge pile of garbage, equivalent to two or three pick-up truck loads. The Crandalls were shocked, and told me they had a sense of foreboding about the transaction. But they still didn't know what they were in for.

At the closing, they learned that the sellers had come earlier and signed the closing documents. According to Jeremy, it was because they were completing the cleanup of the home, and hauling away the offending garbage before they left town. They had people scheduled to assist, and that made it necessary for them to sign early. Jeremy represented that "everything has been taken care of. It's all right." Feeling somewhat reassured, the Crandalls went through with the closing, got the keys and drove to their new home.

You've probably guessed that the pile of garbage was untouched. Nor were the sellers around. It was clear they had packed up and left. The garbage would be left for the Crandalls to deal with. Then they went inside. The stove and refrigerator, two items that, according to the contract, were to remain in the house, had been taken. The heating system and several of the inspection items had not been repaired. And, to add insult to injury, the house had not been cleaned at all.

Attempts to get Jeremy to respond were fruitless. And although I suggested they had some recourse—filing a complaint both with the Realtors® association and with the Real Estate Commission—the Crandalls eventually took the route of least resistance, cleaned up, performed their own repairs, replaced the missing appliances and went on with their lives.

It was too bad. But, unfortunately, most unsatisfactory transactions end up the same way, with no one held accountable, no complaints filed, and buyers left with bitter memories and simply a resolution not to let it happen next time.

Part One

The Home-buying Process, A Brief History

1. A Scenario Under the Old Rules

In the spring of 1998, we decided to combine a summer vacation with hunting for a second home. We initially found you through the Internet and immediately connected with your approach. Our intent was to only look at homes during this trip, not to buy one. You showed us the entire inventory available in our price range. We ended up buying a lovely home in a nice wooded subdivision. Throughout the offer and negotiation process, it seemed like you were reading our minds, because your suggestions were almost exactly what we had decided. This convinced us that you were working for us and that the buyer's broker concept really works.

—Charlie and Nancy Gardner

Prior to 1994, if you wanted to buy a house in Colorado, you might respond to an ad, meet with that Realtor®, see his listing, and if that didn't work out, look at more homes.

Perhaps you'd spend two or three days together looking at homes before you walked into that perfect property. During that time, you and "your" Realtor® became friendly, told jokes, shared stories, and probably had a meal or two together. And when it was time to make the purchase, you knew you were working with a friend, and you got the distinct feeling that the Realtor® was working for you.

And you were wrong!

You see, in those days the law of the land as far as real estate transactions were concerned was called "**the law of sub-agency.**" Under the law of sub-agency, that

Realtor® (with very few exceptions) worked for the seller and he had an obligation to try to get the **Seller** the best deal possible.

The Realtor's only obligation to you was to provide information you may have requested about the house, the neighborhood, etc. If you didn't think, for example, to ask to see what other homes in the neighborhood had sold for, the Realtor® wouldn't have to show you. He was always obligated under State law to let you know of any material defects in the house that he was aware of (for example, if it was located on expansive soils and had a constant problem with the foundation cracking). But rarely, if ever, did a Realtor® recommend ways for you to benefit during the sale, such as getting the seller to pay your closing costs or helping you with other financing options.

The bottom line was that **you were on your own!**

2. Why Sellers Always Got the Best Deal

Over the past three years, you have represented us in two purchases and one sale. You even helped in the sale of some property in another area. Your advice has always been insightful, honest and to the point. From our first purchase, a tiny condominium, we have gradually moved up 'til we are now in a detached home with plenty of room and great views. We can't imagine buying a home without a buyer's representative and very much appreciate your participation in our efforts.

—Leslie Day and John Burnette

Here is how the law of sub-agency worked. It was essentially established when real estate brokers began to share their listings. For years, the only way such brokers could sell a house was to contact everyone they knew and to advertise. A home seller would then try to identify a broker who knew the most people or was really effective at advertising. It was often like finding a needle in a haystack.

Broker associations were usually not very well organized, and even state laws governing real estate sales were, in many cases, somewhat primitive. Occasionally, one or more brokers would get together over coffee or a meal and share their listings. They might make a handshake agreement that if one broker brought in a buyer for another's listing, the commission would be shared.

Then, some years ago, enterprising Realtors® with the National Association of Realtors® decided it would be beneficial to formalize the sharing of listings. This would benefit not only the Realtors®, but the sellers as well. By implication, buyers would also benefit. This was the genesis of the **multilist** systems (the MLS).

With the advent of the MLS, all Realtors® who wanted to participate would put all of their listings in a central databank, which usually resulted in a book, issued periodically, that any Realtor® could peruse. But, participation resulted in several things:

!. In the early 1990s, as a result of two court cases (*Little v. Rohauer* and *Stoertron v. Beneficial Finance*), the Colorado Supreme Court held that, as a matter of law, licensees represented the seller unless they had a written letter or a contract to the contrary.

2. Since only a few buyer brokers had any sort of writing to the contrary, we had a market full of seller agents.

3. Most Realtors®, as a result, ended up representing the seller even if the property was listed by another Realtor®.

This last point is very important. It makes clear that Realtors® almost always saw themselves as representatives of sellers. It was their mission in life. And they pursued it with a zeal unequaled in many professions.

And even though the Colorado Real Estate Commission required real estate licensees to disclose to a buyer that they represented the seller, it was rarely disclosed.

Generally, they would tell the seller anything they learned about you, including your ability to pay more, your willingness to pay more, and your motivations for making the purchase.

You might feel certain that you were working with a friend when you looked at those homes. But the bottom line was that he was always representing the seller—and keeping you in the dark about it. And more often than not, you were betrayed!

So, when you were ready to make the offer, you would typically ask "your" Realtor® something like, "How low an offer do you think the seller would accept?" And he could legally only answer, "I'll submit whatever offer you want to make." You had to figure it out for yourself.

And when "your" friendly Realtor® presented the offer? The seller might say, "Well, the offer seems pretty low. How high do you think they will go?" And the Realtor® might respond, "Well, they told me they wouldn't go over $100,000." And the seller would say, "Good, let's counter at that." As a result, lots of buyers paid more for homes than they had to. Perhaps you were one of them.

3. How the Rules Started Changing

You have provided services as a buyer broker for several of my real estate transactions. In each instance, you well represented my interests. I confirmed my first purchase without seeing it and while living in Florida, based on videotape you took of the property and furnished to me. When I moved here, I saw the home for the first time, and it confirmed that, working as a team, we made a perfect choice for my needs. I subsequently purchased a prime investment property because of your exceptional diligence. A facsimile announcement of the property's availability was sent to your office about 5 p.m., and I was able to submit a contract within two hours. I don't know of another attorney who would have as much faith in another professional as I have had in you. I am extremely pleased with every transaction I have completed with you.

—Dee Phelps

Now, it is important to know that this one-sided negotiating did not all happen in a vacuum. Buyers and sellers who felt cheated or defrauded complained, legislatures responded with tougher laws, and State regulatory agencies became more and more involved in the oversight of real estate practice.

The federal government also heard the cries. In 1983, the Federal Trade Commission (FTC) conducted a national survey of recent buyers of real estate to determine how they felt about their transactions. The results were nothing short of astounding. The FTC survey found that approximately two-thirds of all buyers surveyed thought they were being represented in the transaction when, in fact, they were not.

It became agonizingly clear that the lack of disclosure to buyers about the process was having a negative effect on the reputation of the real estate profession as a whole. Buyers were losing faith in the process, and with good reason. They were getting trod upon, taken advantage of, and in many cases, harmed financially. Lawsuits were being filed by consumers across the country against real estate licensees.

To their credit, there were many in the profession who did not feel that the existing process was fair. Realtors® were beginning to realize the importance of representing buyers, and developed contracts to do just that.

Buyer agency sprung from the determination of a small number of independent thinking, gutsy, radical Realtors®. With a contract in hand to represent a buyer, they would peruse the MLS, show properties, and make offers. Those offers started changing substantially from the norm. They would often include concessions from the seller—closing costs, financing points and other items paid by the seller on behalf of the buyer, lower prices, carpet and fix-up allowances, and so on.

And traditional seller's agents began to take notice. Those who strongly supported the status quo often fought buyer's agents. They would present the offer, then often create animosity in the negotiation process, but let it go to contract. Then, at closing, they would keep all the commissions and refuse to compensate the buyer's Realtor®.

Many Realtors® operating as buyer's agents had to plead their cases in arbitration through the state Realtor® association or take the case to court in order to collect their fair share of the commission (called the cooperative fee split).

The National Association of Realtors® discussions often became heated between traditionalists who didn't

want to see the rules change and new-thinking, progres-
sive Realtors® who felt change was necessary. The profession of real estate was evolving. But, as with anything
that encompasses hundreds of thousands of members,
and hundreds of local, state and national associations, it
was experiencing a great deal of conflict in the process.

The Colorado Association of Realtors® recognized the
importance of the discussion, and joined with the Colorado Real Estate Commission to research the issues. In
1993, when legislation was introduced in the Colorado
legislature to change agency laws, it was supported by
both the Association and the Commission.

And on January 1, 1994, a new agency law went into
effect in Colorado putting buyers on equal footing with
sellers. One attorney has called this the death of "Agency
by Surprise."

Part Two

A New Law for the People

4. What is Agency, Anyway?

We learned a lot about buyer agency working with
you. When you showed us everything in the
county in our price range, and we couldn't find
anything we liked, that didn't stop you. You
found us a home that was not listed, was not being advertised, and that even the owner didn't
know he was going to sell. But it went together so
easily. Even when we were back home in California getting ready for the move, you took care of
the details. Then you helped introduce us to people in our new community and supported us in
our new career. You are the best!

—Larry and Lorrie Keen

An Obligation Conferred

First of all, it is important to understand agency. It's easy
to banter about words like *sub-agency* and *real estate agency*,
but the fact of the matter is that *agency* is a legal term. Its
use confers a legal obligation—and, perhaps, some legal
liability.

Let's say, for example, that your parents are going to
be away on a vacation for an extended period of time.
While they are gone, they want someone to deposit their
checks, pay their bills, and carry on business for them as
usual. What they want, in fact, is someone to keep their
best interests in mind and to act accordingly. They ask
you to represent them, to handle all the paperwork for
them in their absence. In order for you to perform those
functions for them legally, they would have to sign a document giving you power to act for them in those matters.

21

This document is called a *power of attorney*, and it makes you their *agent*, or their legal representative.

If you were to call your parent's banker in their absence and ask the banker to transfer money from one account to another, the banker would refuse—unless you can prove that you are the *agent* of your parents. In order to do that, you would have to provide their banker with a copy of the power of attorney.

It is also important to understand that the person empowered to be an agent is in a better position to handle his client's business than the client is. The *agent* is either physically in a better location to handle business for the client, or the agent is more knowledgeable about the matters to be handled than the client is. You hire an attorney—and the attorney becomes your agent—because the attorney understands law and you do not.

The same is true when working with real estate professionals. In the past, when Realtors® almost always represented sellers, they were the *agents* of those sellers, and other Realtors® they "hired" through the MLS became the sellers' *sub-agents*. As a consequence, all of the Realtors® involved had a legal obligation to represent the best interests of the seller in every transaction. Now, it could be argued that they also had an obligation to be honest with buyers, to disclose their relationship with sellers. But I believe most Realtors® felt this might compromise the interests of the seller, and it justified their silence.

So, in fact, buyers of real estate in the era of *sub-agency* were at a disadvantage, not because they were always dealing with lying or unscrupulous Realtors®, but because the rules were made with sellers in mind, and the sellers were always represented. But we should never lose sight of the fact that Realtors® have always felt that, in order to be successful, they have to take listings (list properties for sale under contracts with sellers)—and the one with the most listings wins. So, every property listing they took made them an agent of that seller. And every action they took in the process of marketing the seller's home had to keep the seller's interests in mind. Is it any wonder that buyers felt cheated?

Now, let's change the rules. The 1994 law introduced a new term to real estate, called *single agency*. Under *single agency*, a seller could be represented by one Realtor® (*agent*), and a buyer could be represented by another Realtor® (*agent*). All at once, some balance was potentially brought to the transaction. I say potentially, because everyone had to learn the new rules. Some Realtors® made the transition easily and happily, and some did not. There was, and still is, some resistance in the real estate community to buyer's agents. It is diminishing over time. Transactions are becoming less adversarial, and both buyers and sellers are feeling more fairness in the deals they make.

Vicarious Liability

There is one other aspect of agency that merits discussion, and that is the existence of *vicarious liability*. Most people understand that a liability is a risk. It's an exposure. You take on a liability when you hire an attorney to take actions on your behalf. If that attorney signs a contract on your behalf which creates an unattractive obligation to a third party, you are still liable for your attorney's actions. Or, your child could damage the property of another, and you might be held responsible for reparations. That is *vicarious liability*. It is extending your risk through reliance on or responsibility for others.

Every time you engage an agent to represent you, you take on some vicarious liability. (Remember the buyer whose agent recommended an uninsured home inspector? The buyer paid the price.) You rely on your agent to make decisions and recommendations on your behalf that are, in fact, in your best interest. And you have engaged that agent because you believe his knowledge in the arena is certainly greater than yours and, you hope, greater than others in the same field.

Many lawsuits have been filed against agents by their clients for failure to act in a professional or prudent manner, or for otherwise putting the client unnecessarily at risk. When a client suffers a loss as a result of the agent's actions, that client will usually feel a need to be compensated for that loss. However, lawsuits are expensive, and many who have suffered losses do not file complaints.

Historically, the vast majority of lawsuits filed have involved seller's agents. There are so many ways that a seller's agent can misrepresent a property and obligate a seller for the agent's misrepresentations. There are very few instances, however, when a buyer's agent can misrepresent a buyer such that the buyer is put at risk. Nevertheless, even when retaining a Realtor® to represent you as your buyer's agent, you need to be aware that there may be some vicarious liability. And it will behoove you to ensure that your agent is experienced, knowledgeable, professional and willing and able to work for you.

5. What Happened in Colorado?

You are the second Realtor® I worked with under a
contract. But you listened to what I wanted and
didn't waste my time showing me homes that
didn't fit my needs. You have my recommendation as one of the hardest working Realtors®.

—Tammy Lupiezowietz

Under the old rules, Realtors® participating in a Multi-
ple Listing Service always represented the seller unless a
written agreement existed to the contrary. This, in spite of
the fact that most buyers believed they were working with
"their agent," and that "their agent" owed them all the
normal fiduciary duties, loyalty and confidentiality. One
Colorado attorney, G. Lane Earnest, described this situation in 1986 as "agency by surprise" in a discussion about
the disclosure dilemma in real estate transactions. In fact,
the situation garnered increased attention in law publications and in the courts.

The response, though long in coming, was dramatic
and actually quite thorough. Legislation passed in 1993
(Senate Bill 93-223) addressed the concerns of consumers
who felt both non-represented and mis-represented, and
in one fell swoop changed the rules of the game. The legislation was actually fueled by movements within the profession. The National Association of Realtors® had
responded to the 1983 Federal Trade Commission survey
and to growing concern by its Realtor members by
changing its policy to make sub-agency an optional,
rather than a mandatory, component of MLS participation. Also, the Colorado Real Estate Commission had
formed a task force to study brokerage practices and
dilemmas created by agency issues. This task force actu-

ally developed the recommendations for the legislation with assistance from the Colorado Association of Realtors® and from the Colorado Bar Association.

The law (§12-61-804, Colo.Rev.Stat.) went into effect on January 1, 1994, and set out the obligations owed to consumers by single agents representing the seller or landlord and by single agents representing the buyer or tenant. The law also provided two methods by which a real estate broker could handle "in-house" listings being sold to "in-house" buyers. The broker could either be a *dual agent* or a *transaction broker*.

Single Agency

By far the most important aspect of the new law was that it fleshed out and defined the single agency relationship. It established some procedures and indicators by which one could tell if the relationship was there. In other words, it set up the procedure whereby a single agent could represent a buyer or tenant and another single agent could represent a seller or landlord, and it outlined the obligations and responsibilities of each. Buyer agents are now required to:

- exercise reasonable skill and care on behalf of the buyer;

- promote the buyer's interests with the utmost good faith, loyalty and fidelity;

- disclose to the buyer any known adverse material defects of any property which the buyer intends to purchase;

- counsel the buyer as to those benefits and risks of the transaction actually known to the broker;

- advise the buyer to seek expert assistance where needed;

- account in a timely manner for money and property; and

- inform the buyer of the exposure to vicarious liability for the acts and omissions of agents working on the buyer's behalf.

For the first time, buyers were going to be informed consumers, and the law required it. It would remain to be seen how well it worked in practice.

Dual Agency

Dual agency is not actually a new term, but its use poses a hurdle that many feel is impossible to overcome. It requires that the broker simultaneously be an agent for, and advocate for, both buyer and seller in the transaction. Many feel this creates conflicting allegiances. Opponents of the legislation believed consumers would be the losers in these situations. Now, think about it for a moment. If you are a buyer, and the Realtor® is your agent, and he is giving you advice, what form would it take? Something like, "At $200,000, this house is priced high. I wouldn't offer more than $170,000"? And then, when presenting the offer to the seller, for whom the Realtor® is also an agent and an advocate, does he then say, "This offer is ridiculously low. I'd counter around $195,000"? Seems rather ridiculous, doesn't it? What may, in fact, happen is that the broker gives advice to neither side and says, simply, "you decide." Or, insidious as this may seem, suppose the broker thought of the seller as an old friend, and the buyer as a stranger who walked in the door. However, the draftsmen of the new law recognized that there would continue to be brokers who would never give up advocacy for their sellers and viewed dual agency as one possible solution when a buyer agent sells an in-house listing. And the Colorado Legislature concurred.

Some protection is still built in for both the buyer and the seller, because the dual agent may not disclose to either party without the prior consent of the other: (1) the fact that the buyer may pay more or the seller may take less; (2) the motivating factors for either party; (3) the fact that the buyer or seller would agree to different financial terms; (4) any facts or suspicions about circumstances which potentially represent a psychological stigma on the property; or (5) any material information about the other party unless non-disclosure would constitute fraud or dishonest dealing.

Transaction Brokerage

Transaction brokerage was a completely new concept; it provided a radical, and sometimes workable, method of handling in-house transactions. It is defined in the Colorado legislation as:

> . . . a broker who assists one or more parties throughout a contemplated real estate transaction with communication, interposition, advisement, negotiation, contract terms and the closing of such real estate transaction without being an agent or advocate for the interests of any party to the transaction.

Transaction brokerage requires a step back from the agency relationship to both parties—to neutrality. The arrangement is formalized by the attachment of a "transaction broker addendum" to the buyer-agency and listing contracts. For buyers, sellers and brokers who understand

and can actually make that shift, it makes the in-house transaction work. Your Realtor®, in his representation of you, the buyer, has an obligation to show you properties that fit your needs, desires and financial abilities. If an in-house listing fits, you should be shown the listing. If you want to purchase that property, your Realtor® then lets you determine how to construct the offer and simply carries it back and forth between you and the seller until the two of you reach agreement. The same neutral attitude is carried through each step of the process until the sale is closed.

I feel, however, that transaction brokerage is carried too far in the real world. The legislature didn't limit its use to in-house transactions. First, any buyer who decides not to enter into a buyer-agency contract with a Realtor®, but still chooses to work with that Realtor®, must understand that the Realtor® is, in fact, a transaction broker. That is, the Realtor® is obligated to be neutral, and while he can provide factual information regarding the properties you see, he is not your agent and cannot advocate for you. He is limited by your instructions in the professional advice he can give. If you are not completely familiar with real estate transactions, contracts and other documents, and if you do not know the market thoroughly, you need to recognize that **this relationship can be a serious detriment to your ability to strike the best deal**—particularly when you are relying on the broker's knowledge of the market. Unfortunately, the vast majority of Realtors® have chosen not to be buyer agents, but to practice transaction brokerage only. As a policy, this offers better protection to broker owners of real estate offices, since it relieves brokers of many of the obligations which come with buyer representation.

Under a buyer agent contract, each agent has an obligation to insure that your needs are met. There is an obligation to try to make sure you see all the properties available that fit your parameters until you've made a decision to buy. He will generally advise you as to whether particular issues are good or bad for you, while a transaction broker typically cannot.

Transaction brokerage was touted as a realistic method of filling the gap between what became the outmoded concept of sub-agency and straight buyer agency. It was also recognized as a viable alternative to dual agency and the legal dilemmas posed by that relationship in in-house transactions.

Compensation

Since commissions in this country have historically been paid out of the proceeds of the sale, it has been presumed that the seller is actually paying those commissions, thus setting up the argument that the Realtor® is working for the seller. Take a look: The sellers list their home with a Realtor® and, in the listing contract, offer to pay some percent as a commission upon the successful sale of the home. The Realtor® then offers a portion of that amount to any Realtor® who brings in the buyer. The presumption has always been that the seller is paying the commission, because the seller signed the listing contract in which the commission obligation was created.

Because the seller was presumed to be paying the commission, the argument was that anyone receiving all or part of that commission was working for the seller. However, there has been another argument that, since the buyer is the one actually bringing the money to the transaction, the buyer is paying the commission. This argument has generally been held by a minority within the profession, however, and not sustained in real life.

The new Colorado law basically eliminated the arguments by stating that any party to a transaction may pay any broker's compensation, and the payment will not create or terminate any agency relationship within that transaction. So payment of commissions to both buyer's and seller's Realtors® could continue to be made as it always had—out of the proceeds of the sale—without creating any argument for agency. In the final analysis, home values are established in this country with real estate commissions factored in as part of the value. That is because home sales have been, and almost always are, handled by Realtors®, and the cost of that handling becomes part of the ultimate sales price and value of the home. Therefore, it becomes a moot point who pays the commission—it is simply part of the home value and paid out of the proceeds of the sale. [Note. Listing commissions amounts or percentages are negotiable, and the form of commission agreed to may vary as well. There is no "standard" or "normal" commission.]

Disclosure

The disclosure requirements in the law originally put the onus on the home buyer to inquire about the types of relationship he could have with a broker, and what each meant. The Colorado Real Estate Commission in its rulemaking authority, however, has made this an affirmative obligation on behalf of the broker. So, when you first meet with a broker, you are to be informed about those different relationships. You have the choice—always. You can make the broker your agent, in which case he is obligated to represent your best interests, or you can make the broker a transaction broker, in which case he is neutral and you make all the relevant decisions. I will discuss the differences at length in a later chapter.

But what you must remember is that if the Realtor® fails to inform you of your choices or attempts to choose for you, he may be doing you a disservice. You should not only know your choices, but you should have a Realtor® willing to discuss them with you.

Part Three

Let's Get Started

6. Playing the Field or Getting Engaged

We can't say enough about working with you. You helped us buy our home long distance before we even moved from the Chicago area, then helped our son buy his first home, then a lot next to us. In every case, you helped with advice, but without pushing us when we couldn't make up our minds. Then you helped us negotiate, recommended a top-notch lender, home inspector and so on. We have always felt you were more a friend than 'just a Realtor®.' Thanks for being with us every step of the way.

—Bob and Jo Ann Clark

So, you're ready to look for a home. Perhaps you've been looking already, sort of as a hobby. I've got one question for you. What Realtor® are you working with?

If you are like many home-buyers, particularly when it's their first time, you may have been calling on ads or for-sale signs, going to open houses, and talking to Realtors® to whom you have been referred. But generally, you have avoided committing to one Realtor®, usually on the basis that you don't want to be pressured, or you're "just not ready."

You may also have found that you are not getting much follow-up from the Realtors® you have seen. Do you wonder why?

Well, it might be helpful to know how Realtors® work, and how you can get the best results working with them. First, just like you, Realtors® have to work for a living. Even though it sometimes seems like they work for free, believe me, they don't.

The number of Realtors® who do not make it in this business is astounding. Fewer than 20 percent hang in there for more than three years. Why? Because they find out how difficult it is to actually make money. It's a *very* competitive field. And if they've been around for a few years, they've learned a few things. One of those things is how to identify someone who is *playing the field*. You know who I mean. It's the prospective buyer, spending a little time with several Realtors®, but not committed to any, and probably not committed to the process of buying a home. Many consumers treat buying real estate just like buying a car. They think if they can keep several brokers on a string wondering who is going to get the business, they can strike a better deal. Nothing could be further from the truth.

You see, the more competent, professional and successful a Realtor® becomes, the more business he has, and the more discriminating he is in how he spends his time. If you spend much time with a Realtor® to whom you are not committed, it will likely be with someone newer to the business or less skilled at negotiating and getting deals to close. This is often the person who is building his business, or who is otherwise counting on his next commission to pay bills. In other words, his motivation may be more to help himself than to help you. There is nothing wrong with working with a new or less experienced broker. But you have to take the whole person into consideration. Enthusiasm, willingness to learn, and a positive attitude go a long way toward compensating for lack of experience. So, there is nothing wrong with that, as long as you are getting good service. But there is one simple way of ensuring the service you get is the best available. Make a decision.

That's all there is to it. You should decide, first, if you are serious about buying a home, or determining if you qualify to do so. Then you should select a Realtor® and enter into an agreement to work with that Realtor® exclusively. It's like getting engaged (but not married). Kind of scary, right? Well, of course. It means you are making a commitment—to the process and to the person. But taking that step will produce much better results in the long run.

If you are working with one Realtor®, and he knows you are not "Realtor® hopping," that Realtor® will become as committed to you as you are to him. He will become "your" Realtor®, and he will be working for you. He will likely work to help you get qualified for financing, and when that "hot" property comes on the market, guess who he is going to call? Believe me, it won't be the person who happened to stop in for an hour last weekend. It will be the buyer to whom he is committed. It will be you. After all, he is *obligated* to bring to your attention any property he can find that fits your needs. If it's a great deal, all the better.

As Realtors®, we have all had occasion to work with people who spend a little time with us, then leave with a comment like, "please call me when that little cabin in the woods becomes available." The thing is, we know they have left the same message with half a dozen other Realtors®. And they are the last ones we will call.

I've sold numerous properties where my buyer was the only person to see the house. I try to check new listings every day, and also watch the classified ads in the newspaper for homes being sold by owners. Sometimes I see a property that is obviously under-priced, or perhaps, "priced for a quick sale." It then becomes a game—try to get my buyer into the property before anyone else sees it, because I know it will go fast. A quick call to the buyer whom the property fits to let him know, "I got one," and we're off, usually writing a contract that day.

I don't get paid until I produce a sale. I've worked with some clients for two years before they bought a home. They either needed to get their finances in order or couldn't find the right home. That's a long time to wait to get paid; but since they worked with me exclu-sively, and I knew they were committed to find a home, I didn't mind how long it took. There is not a lot of loyalty in this business. And there are a lot of short term thinkers—people who will unknowingly lose thousands of future dollars to save a thousand today. You will find that two-way loyalty will pay off. The key is selecting the right agent.

7. How to Select Your Realtor® –Credentials, History, Training and Attitude

"We really would like to thank you for all your understanding and kindness you showed us in a difficult situation. You knew what a traumatic time it was for my family to be moving from an area we had been in and loved for over twenty years. Thank you for your professionalism, knowledge, honesty, energy and above all else, kindness.

—Jeanne M. Brown

Credentials

You've probably noticed that whenever I've used the term *Realtor®* in this book, it is capitalized and the registration mark is used. There is a reason for that. The term *Realtor®* is a trademark of the National Association of Realtors®, and anyone who uses that term as part of his professional identity must be a member, not only of the National Association of Realtors® (NAR), but also of his local and state associations. Anyone who is not a member, but is legitimately working in the real estate profession, is still licensed by his state real estate commission and is either a real estate salesperson or a real estate broker.

When Realtor® is used, however, it means several things. NAR members have training available only to members. They have the benefit of local meetings and state and national conferences where they can network with other Realtors®. Many deals are actually made for buyers and sellers at those events. It all comes with a price.

Members also subscribe to a Code of Ethics, which commits them to conduct their business with a sense of fair play. Members of the public have some recourse, then, when they feel they have been lied to, mistreated, or cheated by a Realtor®. They can file an ethics complaint with the local Realtor® association requesting the Realtor® be disciplined, or a request for arbitration if they feel the Realtor® has actually cheated them out of money. The Grievance Committee and the Professional Standards Committee of the organization handle these complaints. And while a member is not bound to submit to the grievance process when a complaint is initiated by buyers or sellers, most do, since it is a much simpler and less costly method of justice than going to court.

Members have to pay dues, MLS charges and other fees to maintain their membership in good standing, but the bottom line is that they are in a position to provide much better service to you than non-members.

Those who do not have the Realtor® designation are operating independently. They are often not doing enough business to justify the costs involved in belonging. They do not have the benefit of MLS access, and they are not bound by a code of ethics that governs their professional actions.

So, for starters, get a Realtor®. You'll find the designation on their business cards.

History

If you were taking in a roommate or boarder, you would screen that person to see if you are compatible. If you were renting a property, you would take a rental application and check out the renter's references and credit history. If you were going into business with

someone, or hiring someone, you would be smart to conduct a background check. It never hurts to know with
whom you are working. The same is true with a Realtor®.
In one survey of the National Association of Realtors®,
one-third of the respondents said they would not use the
same agent to purchase in the future. That is a high
degree of dissatisfaction.

As consumers, we have a terrible history of picking
professionals—doctors, lawyers and, yes, Realtors®. We
take a referral from a friend, make an appointment, and
that's usually as far as we go. But, if we end up dissatisfied
later, it's our own fault for not taking responsibility for
our own selection. We need to prescreen, ask questions,
get a feel for how compatible we might be, and for how
well that professional can meet our needs.

It is sometimes difficult not to work with a friend in
the business and to select someone else, but it might be
the most valuable decision you could make. I have
known people who have listed their home with a
Realtor® friend who specialized in commercial sales and
never sold a house. Were they feeling sorry for him? You
need to ask some questions before starting with any
Realtor®. Instead of sitting down with a Realtor® and
saying, "We're looking for a house in the $200,000
range," start out with something like, "Before we start,
I'd like to learn a few things about you." Interview your
potential agent, ask questions, and determine the following important issues to your satisfaction.

Get a full-time agent.

Most full-time agents work 50-60 hours a week or
more. They are committed to their work and to their clients. A part-time Realtor® is there to make a deal when it
comes along, but either doesn't need the income a full-
time career will produce (a retiree?) or isn't making it yet
(and may hold two or more jobs). Within reasonable

limits, a Realtor® should fit his schedule to yours, not the other way around.

Get an agent who is busy.

A successful Realtor® is busy and will not be able to spend all day, every day with you. But a couple of half-days a week to look at property is generally sufficient. Again, it depends on your circumstances. If you are only in town for two days, you might need his full attention while you are there. Ask for it.

Ask your potential agent how many sales (called sides) they closed last year and the year before. A "side" is one side of the sale. When one Realtor® had the listing and another one brought in the buyer, each produced one "side." An agent who has closed only four to eight sides in a year is not doing enough business to merit having yours. Either he doesn't need money, just got started, or can't get enough business to survive and is on his way into another profession. An agent who has done 15 or 20 sides is not making a great deal of money but is surviving and probably growing. And believe it or not, he is far above the national average.

An agent who is doing 40, 50 or more sides a year is very busy—usually for a reason. He has attracted business, hopefully because he has served people well, though some Realtors® generate lots of business simply through smart advertising. It is, therefore, important to get a sense of how many transactions were results of referrals from past clients.

Make sure the broker works mostly with buyers.

If you are considering a real estate purchase, make it a top priority to select a Realtor® who has a history of working primarily with buyers. Now that you know how busy the Realtor® is, ask how many of those sides were working with buyers and how many were listings. I would suggest this ratio should be weighted two to one in favor of buyer representation. I'll talk more about credentials below, but if a Realtor® has the ABR designation (Accredited Buyer Representative), he has already taken training specific to buyer representation and has demonstrated a commitment to working with buyers.

Check out the broker's specialty.

If you are looking for a home, select an agent who specializes in residential sales. If you want to buy an apartment building or a business, select a Realtor® who specializes in commercial sales. There are numerous specialties in real estate, and your agent's specialty should be consistent with your goals. Note that in larger metropolitan areas, Realtors® also tend to specialize in geographic areas, in price ranges or with types of buyers. An agent who primarily sells million-dollar homes won't have the time for the $200,000 home-buyer. And some agents specialize in helping first-time home-buyers, while others really don't want the additional responsibility involved.

Make sure the broker is technologically current.

In today's world, it is becoming vitally important that professionals with whom you work are computer literate and have a grasp on some of the new gadgets designed to improve their service to their customers. What does that mean?

First, many states require that Realtors® use certain forms in real estate transactions. These forms are almost always available on computer programs, and this presents the quickest, most accurate way to generate contracts. Realtors® who continue to hand write their contracts, or who use a typewriter to fill in the blanks on standard forms are living in the past, have demonstrated an unwillingness to keep up with the times, and may not be capable of providing the best service.

Other types of software allow Realtors® to track their customer's needs, access increasingly more sophisticated MLS systems, and communicate by electronic mail, or *e-mail.* Digital cameras allow Realtors® to send photos electronically to out-of-area buyers about new listings and hot properties, with interior and view shots all as part of the package.

If the Realtor® you are interviewing is not, at a minimum, able to utilize a computer, beat a hasty retreat. And make sure that when he says he is computerized, he is not just relying on an assistant or a shared secretary to do all his computer work for him. Where will you be if his assistant is not around or is too busy to prepare the contract? You could be waiting while a competing offer takes the property you want.

How is a mutual commitment established?

People who commit to work together usually put the agreement in writing. Does the agent you are interviewing regularly enter into a buyer-agency contract with his buyers? A good agent will generally not work with someone unless there is a mutual commitment—even if it's only for a very short time, enough to determine if you are compatible. That commitment can take the form of a written buyer-agency contract in which your agent agrees to represent you, and you agree to work exclusively with your agent. Or, it could be an exclusive transaction broker contract, if you do not want representation.

I have a friend in the business who will not show property to anyone who has not signed a buyer-agency agreement with him. However, he understands that when he and a potential buyer have just met, they know very little about each other, and there is hesitation about signing a long-term commitment. So, he will suggest they sign the agreement for one day only. And he will tell the buyer that at the end of the day, the buyer will either decide that he wants to work with someone else (in which case the commitment is over), or the buyer can't afford or doesn't want to buy in this market, or the buyer wants to continue working with him (at which time the agreement is extended, usually for several months).

See the next chapter on buyer-agency contracts for a more detailed discussion of this important issue.

Training

Anyone worth his salt in any profession continues to update his knowledge about the work that he does. Doctors, lawyers and mechanics face an ever-changing world when it comes to their professions and must take classes to continue to be of service to their customers. The same is true of Realtors®.

State laws require continuing education. But the requirements are usually minimal; three or four one-day classes every two or three years. Good Realtors® find the time to take much more training than that. There are a number of designations denoting certain continuing education landmarks. They are signified on business cards in the form of letters following the Realtor's name. While some may be in areas not related to residential sales, all show a commitment on behalf of the Realtor® to keep his professional skills honed. And that's good. Do not work with a Realtor® who demonstrates no interest in continuing education. Look for some of the following designations on your prospective agent's business card.

ABR—Accredited Buyer Representative— requires additional training in agency issues and a thorough understanding of what it takes to represent buyers. While your Realtor® does not need this designation to represent you, it denotes his commitment to doing so. Graduates are members of the Real Estate Buyer Agency Council (REBAC) and receive continuing information to keep them informed of new buyer agency issues. While the numbers are growing, the percentage of Realtors® who have this designation is still low. When you find a Realtor® who is an ABR, talk to him. In fact, I recommend that you seek out this designation. It is more important than any other you will see below. It represents a commitment to buyers, and a mindset oriented toward your best interests.

GRI—Graduate Realtor's Institute—represents approximately 80 hours of advanced education beyond the training that is required to be licensed. It is usually the first step to becoming more informed and professional.

CRS—Certified Residential Specialist—requires completion of numerous two-to-three-day classes held around the country. It takes the average Realtor® a few years to complete and usually costs $5,000 to $10,000 in tuition and travel costs. It provides significantly increased and detailed knowledge in residential issues and is the graduate degree of residential sales. Graduates are members of the Residential Sales Council (RSC) and receive continuing information in a variety of ways to keep them abreast of new issues in this area.

ALC—Accredited Land Counselor—similar to the CRS, this usually requires several years and several thousand dollars in costs to achieve. It's the graduate degree in the area of land sales.

CCIM—Certified Commercial Investment Member—like the CRS, this commercial sales designation requires extensive continuing education. Graduates are members of the Commercial Sales Council and are the experts in commercial property sales.

There are many other designations. If you see one you are not familiar with, ask the Realtor® about it. Most Realtors® are proud of their designations and happy to talk about them.

Attitude

I just cannot end this section without a discussion about attitude and disposition. I mentioned that a good, winning attitude makes up for a lot, and it's true. I'd much rather work with a newly-licensed Realtor® who really wants to help than with an old curmudgeon who has been in the profession for years, thinks he knows all the answers and will not listen to anything new. There are a lot of worn-out Realtors® who have "seen it all" still occupying desk space in offices across the land.

Your initial interview with a prospective agent will tell you lots about his approach to life. Work with an optimist, not a pessimist. Listen to his answers to your questions. Is he saying, "There's nothing available in your price range," or is he saying instead, "It might be difficult to find exactly what you want in that price range, but let's look at some properties so you have a better handle on this market."

It isn't brain surgery to figure this out. Look for a good, positive attitude as part of your evaluation process.

8. The Buyer-Agency Contract

When making such an important purchase as real
estate, we would insist that our broker/agent work
for our best interests alone. You worked with us as
our buyer agent and used your experience to find
a house and negotiate the best deal for us in a
tough resort market.

—Daniel and Julie Zangari

Abuyer-agency contract is a contract between the
buyer (you) and the broker, and it works two ways. First,
the Realtor® broker becomes your agent and, as such, is
obligated to represent your best interests. Second, it represents your commitment to the Realtor® and says that you
will work with him exclusively. This means when you see
a sign on a property, you will not call the listing agent yourself to negotiate a deal, nor will you go into a property that
is for-sale-by-owner to do the same. Instead, you will call
your agent and ask him to get you information on the
property. You now have an agent. Use him. The whole purpose of this exercise is to get you the best deal possible. If
you have selected a good agent, you should recognize that
he has the experience and the skills necessary to represent
you effectively. It now takes a modicum of trust to see that
play out, and it is time for your Realtor® to earn the
commission.

There are a few items that you should pay particular
attention to in a buyer-agency contract. In Colorado,
most of these things are already part of the standard contract, but in many other states, this may not be the case.
A sample contract is included in Appendix A. Before you
sign, at least discuss the following:

Confidentiality

It is imperative if you are to be represented effectively, the agent must keep confidential any information which he learns about you. In particular, the fact that you may be able or willing to pay more, or accept concessions, or your motivating factors should not be revealed, except as a valid negotiating tool and with your prior consent.

In addition, you have a right to be assured that confidential information remains confidential even after you have bought your home, or your contract with the Realtor® has expired or been terminated in any way. If you make an offer on an in-house transaction (where the seller is also represented by the brokerage that is representing you), information about you should remain just as confidential as when you are negotiating for a property listed by another firm.

Scope of Work

The contract will contain a description of what type of property your Realtor® is instructed to seek for you. Make sure it fits what you want. If you are looking specifically for a residence, make sure the language limits the search to that. Do not accept language that says "any property." If you are considering purchasing a home from a family member or friend, you may ask to have that property excluded from the contract. However, you may want to ask your Realtor® what he would charge to handle that transaction for you. Pitfalls can still exist and, in fact, they can be more serious and more heart-wrenching when dealing with someone close to you. Many close relationships have been damaged or ruined when friends and relatives have done business together. It's usually not because of a lack of good intentions. It happens because objectivity is lost, personal feelings get exaggerated and hurt, and the process erodes. I've worked on numerous deals where family members and close friends were involved, and have found that it became vitally important to ensure that the deal was a win/win for everyone involved.

Compensation

This is the time, not later, to determine how your Realtor® gets paid. There are a variety of ways this can occur. You can agree to pay your Realtor® a flat fee at closing, an hourly fee, a commission based on how much the Realtor® saves you from the listing price, or you can agree to any number of other strategies.

There is an option, however, which is generally accepted, and which most buyers find more acceptable than putting money out-of-pocket: Your Realtor® gets paid out of the proceeds of the sale at closing. Keep in mind that the listing Realtor® is being paid a commission, which is described in the listing contract with the seller. The listing Realtor® then typically offers half of that commission to another Realtor® who might bring in the buyer for the property. That compensation, called the "co-op" or cooperative fee split, is paid to your Realtor® at closing. If you were to select one of the other compensation choices above, that co-op would be credited to you at closing.

If your Realtor® is to be paid at closing based on a percentage of the purchase price of the home, it is doubly important that you have a Realtor® who you feel will put your best interests in front of his own.

What about for-sale-by-owner properties? I spell out the exact commission to be paid in those cases, and the commission is written into the offer to purchase. When the contract is submitted to the owner, the commission is included in the discussion. There are times when a seller being represented by a Realtor® refuses to pay a buyer-agent. This is rare, but there are still people out there, and some Realtors®, who look at buyer-agents as

the enemy. In a case like this, you and your Realtor®
should have a discussion to determine how payment will
work, or if it is even worth it for you to negotiate for that
house. I include language in our buyer-agency contracts
to accommodate this, and it would be wise to discuss this
up front.

In any event, keep in mind that your Realtor®, unlike
most professionals who get retainers or charge by the
hour, does not get paid until a property is closed (unless
you have agreed to another arrangement). Every Realtor®
works deals that never close, and they do not get paid for
those. Also, home values across the country are established historically with a real estate commission
included. That means that a part of the purchase price is
almost always paid to a Realtor® for professional services.
An appraisal of value does not separate one from the
other.

Length of the Contract, Cancellation

I typically write buyer agency contracts for six
months, which is a long time. But, I often work with
buyers of second homes, and the buying process involves
communicating with buyers when they are in their
home state or city. So, I will coordinate property show-
ings with their vacations to my area. Sometimes my
buyers buy properties I have recommended sight unseen.
But even when working with locals, I use a six-month representation period.

This long a period can be scary. What if you decide
you do not like your agent? What if your plans change?
The simplest answer to this is to ask for a cancellation
clause. I always include a clause that says either party
(you or me) may cancel the contract for any reason what-
soever by providing written notice to the other party of
that decision. I ask for a ten-day advance notice. But I
believe that you can't force people to work together who

are not compatible. If your Realtor® is willing to give you this "out" in your contract, you can bet he is fairly confident of his ability to represent you effectively. Keep in mind that you would not be able to cancel a contract for a property on which you are already negotiating. And every contract will have what is called a "holdover" clause. That means that if, after terminating the contract with your Realtor®, you go back to a property you saw with that Realtor® and buy it, he may be entitled to a commission.

The entire contract should be designed to be fair to both parties. It is fair to be able to cancel a contract when two people cannot work together. It is not fair to have someone do a lot of work for you and then cancel. You should be able to determine in the first or second meeting with your Realtor® whether or not you are compatible. Don't spend several weeks or months together and then decide to go with someone else.

In-House Transactions

There are various ways to handle in-house transactions. There are some brokerage firms that only represent buyers. They never take a listing. Their belief is that they are the truest buyer representatives, that their business is uncluttered with seller representation. That may be true, but I tend to believe that the individual is more important than the company. While a Realtor® must work within the philosophy and policies of his brokerage, an agent who meets all the criteria discussed in the previous chapter will serve you well regardless of what company he works for or the policies by which he is bound.

After you have purchased your home, you may also decide in the future to sell it. Naturally, if you had a good experience with your Realtor® in the purchase, you would want to consider the same person to help you sell your house. So, it's always good to keep your options open. Ultimately, you get to decide what is more important—the agent or the company philosophy.

If your Realtor's brokerage also takes listings, your Realtor® will want to show you any of those listings that fit your parameters. If he didn't do so, you might be upset later when you find that you never got to see what might have been the perfect home. When your Realtor® shows you a home where he or another Realtor® in his firm represents the seller, you sometimes have "dual agency" as explained in Chapter Five. Dual agency is where the Realtor® actually represents and advocates for both parties. There are lots of deals done throughout the country using dual agency.

I prefer the following alternative, however, also discussed in Chapter Five: The Colorado legislature, in its wisdom, has defined another relationship called *transaction brokerage*. Other states have adopted the term *facilitator*. A *transaction broker* or *facilitator* is legally obligated to be neutral and objective and to help facilitate the transaction. You are working with a Realtor®, but the Realtor® does not represent you. The Realtor® is not your agent and cannot negotiate on your behalf unless you very specifically direct that negotiation. He is, however, obligated to provide you with all the factual information regarding the property which would normally be provided, or which you might request. While this is not generally a good type of relationship for all transactions, it works for in-house transactions where a relationship has been established between you and your Realtor®, and you have gotten some sense from that relationship of how you might structure an offer. Look at the Transaction-Broker Addendum, which is included as part of the Buyer-Agentr Contract in Appendix A.

I attach a transaction-broker addendum to all of my buyer-agency contracts and my listing contracts. So, whenever an in-house negotiation begins (with the preparation and submission of the offer), the relationship immediately converts to transaction brokerage. You might want to ask if this type of relationship is available in your state or in the firm in which your Realtor works.

So, when the contract establishing the relationship between you and your Realtor® is done, it's time to start looking for a home.

Part four

Getting Your Home

9. Getting the Money

The creative financing you recommended not only allowed us to qualify for more house than we thought we could afford, but will save us thousands in tax credits each year. Thanks for working with us so long. Your patience and willingness to work with us paid off.

—Kent and Julie Brown

Real estate is such a great investment! There is probably nowhere else where you can leverage so much with so little. You can purchase a $100,000 home with $3,000. And if that home goes up in value $10,000 (or 10%) in a year, you've more than tripled your $3,000 investment (333%). Sound too good to be true? It's not. People do it every day. The best place to start investing in life is in your personal residence. If you are renting—stop! Stop now! Renting is a losing proposition. All the money goes out and none comes back to you. If you own your home, you get the advantage of an appreciating asset (it grows in value), and you get the tax advantage of getting to deduct the interest portion of your payment. I'll talk more about this later; but for now, let's talk about how to get the majority of the money to buy your home from someone else.

Now there are times when your dad or your aunt or uncle will finance your home for you. But most people use a finance company—the lender. The lender is probably the second most important member of your team after your Realtor®. Make sure you have a lender that specializes in providing loans for the type of purchase you are making. If you are buying a home, you will use a residential mortgage lender—the loan you obtain on your home is typically called a *mortgage*. If you are buying a business, you will need a commercial lender. And if you are buying land, with certain exceptions, you will probably use a bank. A mortgage lender can do land loans if you are buying a lot and planning to build a home on it immediately. Many mortgage companies now offer what is called a "one-time close, construction-to-perm" loan, which will help you finance the land purchase, provide the construction financing, and then provide the permanent financing once the home is built.

Keep in mind that, in many states, including Colorado, mortgage lenders are not licensed. So, anyone can get into the business; you need to be extra diligent in selecting your lender and your loan officer.

A loan officer is much like a Realtor® in that you may be referred to one by a friend, may have a family member in the business, or happen to meet one by accident. Just remember that not all loan officers are alike. A good Realtor® will have a short list of lenders and loan officers who have proven that they know what they are doing, only make promises they can keep, are known for not having last minute surprises, have a substantial menu of loans to cover most situations, and whose rates and costs are competitive. Last minute surprises are things like finding out a day or two before you are supposed to close on your home purchase that the underwriter is requiring a list of conditions which will be impossible to meet prior to closing, or is denying your loan.

I keep a list of lenders who meet my criteria. And I have gone a step further. Whenever I can, I negotiate with those lenders to waive certain fees for my buyers. Usually, lenders will waive the loan processing fee (which can be anywhere from $150 to $450) if they know they will get regular referrals from a Realtor®.

A good Realtor® will also be familiar with the basics of loan processing and the types of loans available, so he can provide guidance as you work with the lender, and can tell if the person you are working with is knowledgeable. Most Realtors®, however, simply refer you to a lender and stay completely out of the process. I feel that teamwork will get more deals done, so I tend to stay involved to the point of brainstorming unique possibilities with my buyers and their lenders.

married or not?

I worked with a young couple a few years ago who were attempting to purchase their first home. They were not married. The problem was that he had impeccable credit, but no cash in the bank. She had numerous credit problems in the past, but had enough for the down payment and closing costs in the bank. In our meeting with them and their lender, it was clear that she could not be on the loan. And a condition of certain loans (in this case, it was an FHA loan) is that, if the borrower is to receive a gift of money from another party, that other party has to be a blood relative.

Under the circumstances, there was no way she could give the money to him for this home purchase, no matter how close their relationship was. So I suggested one way to make this work—they could get married. The lender said, "Yes, that would work." But the couple, looking a bit chagrined, said in fact, they were planning to get married, but not for another several months. "That's OK," we suggested, "just don't tell anybody. Do it quietly at the courthouse, then have your ceremony with your friends when you had planned." That's exactly what they did, and they were in their new home when they got married. This couple, by the way, has since traded up twice—to the home of their dreams.

Are Better Rates Real?

In a contrasting example, a recent first-time home-buyer started out with a lender I had recommended. Then he read an ad placed in the Denver newspaper by a lender who promised very low interest rates under a new program. My client decided he wanted to switch his loan to this lender. My clients always have the right to choose their own lenders, but I will caution them when I am not familiar with a lender they choose. I let them know that I cannot vouch for that lender's service, competence or knowledge. I do, however, interview the lender to try to determine the viability of the loan program they are offering and to get a sense of how well that lender can represent my client.

In this case, I confirmed that the loan program, while new, was legitimate. It was an adjustable rate loan, which started at a very low interest rate, then increased to market rate over time. There were some pitfalls to the loan, and I made sure my client understood them. I made the lender send me a "good faith estimate" and my buyer decided to proceed. The lender was very positive about my client's qualifications, and assured everyone that this loan would be a "slam dunk." However, the lender could not get the loan processed in time, and we had to extend the contract once. Then, two days before the extended closing, the lender called my client to tell him his loan had been denied, then offered to switch him to another loan with a very high interest rate.

My client called in horror, completely frustrated, and afraid that he had lost his dream home. I called the lender I first recommended, the one he had started with, got my buyer to provide them with a copy of all his paper-work, and in less than 48 hours, that lender got him complete and unconditional loan approval—at conforming rates. While the seller was getting angry over the extensions, we were able to convince his listing Realtor that another short extension was better than seeking another offer on the house. The sale closed the following week and my buyer is now a happy homeowner.

Pre-Qualification and Pre-Approval

Once you have selected a lender, the first thing he should do is pre-qualify you for your home purchase. In other words, the lender will check your credit, get basic information from you on your income and debts, and be able to tell you approximately how much of a mortgage you can qualify for. More and more, lenders are also able to perform what is called "desktop underwriting." That is, if your credit is good enough, and if it appears that your income and debt ratios will work, the lender can submit a loan application immediately by computer, and receive, almost immediately, an answer from the underwriter. Usually, it will come in the form of full loan approval up to a certain loan amount subject to an appraisal of value on the property, or with certain conditions which have to be met (such as verification of the information submitted).

If the lender's pre-qualification does not allow you to buy a home which you feel is suitable, you could ask if you can increase your purchasing power by having your parents co-sign for you, by taking in partners, or by getting down payment assistance from friends, relatives or government programs. You could also ask if the lender has other, non-traditional, loan programs which would allow a higher purchase price. For example, there is a program which allows better rates for home purchases when the home meets certain requirements for energy efficiency.

Note that when you enter into a contract to purchase a home, there will be a deadline by which you must have full loan approval. If you do not obtain full loan approval by the contract deadline, you may terminate the contract. If you do not terminate the contract, you will be obligated to purchase the home or lose your earnest money deposit. That means, of course, that you must be working with a lender you can trust, and you must ensure that you do not spend the money you will be required to bring to the closing table.

When you and your Realtor® have established your relationship with a mortgage lender and established your purchase limits, you can embark on a home search where you will only be looking at properties you can realistically afford.

The Good Faith Estimate

A good faith estimate is a form your lender provides you that shows several things. It shows the lender's regular charges, along with the other anticipated closing costs involved with the loan. It utilizes those figures to estimate the total amount of cash you will need to buy your house and calculates your approximate monthly payment. Some lenders will insist they cannot provide a good faith estimate until you have a property under contract or in escrow. That's baloney. Good faith estimates are simply that—estimates—and they can be prepared quickly and easily. In fact, some lenders I work with will prepare several, one for each loan scenario they are discussing with you. It assists you in comparing those loans so you can decide which to take.

It also gives you something to compare with other lenders if you happen to be shopping for the best rates and costs. If one lender charges, for example, a $450 loan processing fee, and another charges $150, and the rates and other fees are the same, you might want to spend more time with the lender who charges less. But do not let these fees be the only reason for selecting a lender. A good mortgage broker is worth their weight in gold.

You should also get a good faith estimate on two other occasions—(1) when you have a property under contract, and your Realtor® provides a copy of that contract to the lender; and (2) when you change loan programs, either because you don't qualify for the one you started with, or you decide on a different plan. Once you are under contract, many of the items which were estimated on the first good faith estimate are known, so the *estimate* is more accurate and closer to reality.

The Last-Minute Fees

Occasionally, one of our clients decides to use a lender I haven't recommended. In one case, a couple decided to work with a lender who was renting a home from this couple's parents. The lender promised to cut his origination fee in half because of the relationship. Usually, a lender charges a 1.0% loan origination fee. That fee is generally split between the loan officer and the mortgage company he works for. In this case, the lender either gave up his portion of that fee, or worked it out with his boss for the company to discount the deal. At any rate, when I compared his good faith estimate with other lenders, the reduced fee made the difference. Their loan was going to be about $140,000, so a 1.0% fee would have been $1,400. They saved $700 by going with this lender, all other things being equal.

I met with the lender and told him that, if he really took care of our clients, he would get other referrals from me. Since he was just getting established in the area, he was eager for the new business. However, it took him longer to process the loan than he thought, and I did not have a settlement statement until the actual day of closing. I called him and the title company to bring something to their attention—the fact that there was a 1.0% loan origination fee on the statement rather than .5%–and asked for a correction. But this loan officer insisted he had met with my clients, and that because they had not locked in their rates, and rates had gone up somewhat, he took a full origination fee rather than increase the rate.

I asked to see the new good faith estimate that he should have provided if this were true. He said he did not provide one, but that my clients understood the new loan terms. My clients insisted there was no such agreement, and at the closing table, they were faced with a dilemma. They had to close with the charges as they appeared, or get the lender to write them a check back for the .5% difference, or walk away and refuse to close on the home. They closed, and did not get a refund from the lender. They were angry with him but happy to be in their new home. That lender has never received a referral from me, and within a few months, he was out of business, or at least, gone from the area. He certainly does not rent from my clients' parents anymore.

Loan Types and Interest Rates

There are a variety of loan types available, and the loan program you select will depend first on your ability to qualify, and then on your right to select one over another.

There are so many loan variables that it would be impossible to discuss them all here. But be aware that certain loans are specially targeted for first-time homebuyers, and offer features such as low down payment (as little as nothing down), competitive interest rates, and the ability to have a co-signer or receive down payment assistance from another source.

At the time of this writing, second-home loans are available for 10% down with interest rates as low as on primary residences. Investment loans can be obtained for as little as 10% down (though 20% or more is more common), and the interest rates are somewhat higher.

The general rule is that the more risk you ask a mortgage company to assume, the tougher the rules are going to be for the mortgage you want. Government guaranteed loans (e.g., FHA, VA) take some of the onus off the lender, so that they can keep the rules easier for you to meet. But conventional loans (anything not guaranteed by an agency of the federal government) tend to follow this formula. The more money you put down, and the better qualified you are to repay the loan, the more the mortgage company will be willing to give you good terms and rates.

Interest rates today are around the lowest they have been in over 20 years. The political and economic climate in this country have conspired to produce 30-year fixed rates which have hovered near 6.75% to 7.5% for about two years. It's at the point where nearly anyone with decent credit and a job can buy a home. You can't always get exactly what you want the first time. But owning, saving, and taking advantage of a growing market may well give you the ability to take your increased equity every couple of years and trade into a better home. Many of my clients have done just that.

Creative Financing

If you are finding it difficult to get financing through the normal programs, you may have to get creative. Some of the lenders with whom I work like my ideas. For example, with enough money down (usually 20%, but sometimes only 10%), you can get an *NIV loan* or a *no-doc loan*. NIV stands for "no income verification." It is a loan where the lender feels there is a large enough down payment, and hence they would feel relatively secure if you were to default, so they do not concern themselves with verifying the income you state on your loan application. They may simply verify you are employed where you say you are and you actually have the resources necessary to cover the down payment and closing costs. A *no-doc loan* is a loan where the lender does not require documentation of either income or assets (assets in this case means the money to cover down payment and closing costs). Both of these loans will have a higher interest rate, as much as 1.0% to 2.0% higher than conforming loans. But, when you can't do normal financing, these are still good loans to go after.

Many mortgage brokers also have connections for what are called "B" and "C" loans. These are loans with higher, sometimes much higher, interest rates, that are designed for people who cannot qualify for normal financing. They are usually high credit risks.

You may also try to find a seller who is willing to finance part or all of the purchase for you. I have engineered several purchases where the seller only had 10% to put down but needed a 20% down no-doc loan. I would get the seller to carry a second note for the buyer in the amount of 10% of the purchase. Then, with the buyer's additional 10% down, he only needed an 80% primary mortgage. The buyer ended up with two notes to pay off, but the combined payments were usually within a few dollars of what a 90% loan would have been anyway.

I have also identified certain people who have money to invest, and would like to make somewhat more than the going 30-year rate. For 1% or 2% above the prevailing 30 year rate, they are often willing to finance a smaller mortgage themselves. Sometimes, such a loan has a balloon payment, meaning that it has smaller payments for a period of time (like five years), and then at the end of that period, the entire amount becomes due. For people who have had credit problems in the past, but can demonstrate that they are making efforts to clean up their credit, a loan such as this will often get them to the point where they can refinance conventionally, long before a balloon payment becomes due. When a buyer has very little cash to put down, a private lender may take other collateral, such as a car or business equipment, instead.

There are many types of creative financing. All of them carry more risk than normal conventional financing, and most will cost more in terms of interest rates. Most, however, do not have financing costs involved (such as loan origination fees, points, etc.). But sometimes, it's the only way to make a deal work. And if so, you should consider the options. Just make sure you ask lots of questions and have your Realtor® at your side.

Finally, although I have never seen an agreement making your loan officer your "loan agent," you want to work with one who will, in fact, keep your best interests in mind throughout the financing process. So, the best place to start is with the Realtor® you have retained. That Realtor® should be assisting you in this area, as well, from lender recommendations to brainstorming sessions to troubleshooting when there are problems. It all centers on that Realtor® and your ability to make him get you the best deal.

10. Finding the Right Home

What a trip! I was just getting my business, Sweet Peas, off the ground and didn't have lots of time to look for a new home—never mind that it was a necessary activity. You accommodated my schedule so well. Then, after making offers on three— count them, three—homes, I actually got the best of the three for a very good price. As an attorney, I will tell anyone that being represented by a buyer agent is the only way to go. As a business owner, I appreciate the fact that you made sure that all the time we spent together was productive.

—Melanie Kelley

Once you have your relationship established with your Realtor® and you have your lender on board, you can look for a home with a much better perspective on what you can afford. Whether you are a first time home-buyer, looking for a second home, or building your real estate investment portfolio, knowledge brings understanding and control to the process. You will also be in a better position when making an offer, since you are already pre-qualified (possibly even pre-approved) for your loan.

The Search

Your Realtor® will first select homes for you to see from the MLS (the Realtor® Multilist Service). However, a buyer agent is not limited to the MLS. He will probably be aware of new home construction projects, and might peruse the classified ads in the newspaper or otherwise be aware of homes being sold directly by owners. Or, occasionally, he might have knowledge of a home or two that the owners have not absolutely decided to sell, but are considering. In addition, you might see open house signs or other signs on homes that appeal to you. **A word of caution:** You have selected a Realtor and the two of you have an agreement to work together. So, when you see a sign on a house for sale, **do not** call on the sign. Call your Realtor instead and ask him to do the research, let you know the details, and set a showing if appropriate. Also, ask him how you should handle yourself in open houses. Keep in mind that the listing Realtor sitting at the open house, or responding to your telephone inquiry from his sign, is usually representing the seller, and he would like nothing more than to keep a buyer's agent from getting a commission by claiming you as "his" buyer.

The homes selected by your Realtor® should generally encompass your stated parameters, including price range, number of bedrooms and baths, general size, garage and other physical attributes of a home. They will be in your preferred neighborhoods or communities and/or school districts and have other attributes you have indicated are important. As you look, you may find that you cannot put all the things you want together in one package. You can get the home you want, but not in the right school district or neighborhood, and so on. You may have to refine your search several times. If you stick to the price parameters established between you, your lender and your Realtor®, then you will probably have to give up some of your preferences. If you are unwilling to give anything up, then you will have to take another look at financing—bringing in a family member to co-sign, working with a partner, or looking for properties in which the seller will carry all or part of the financing.

Please realize you will most likely not be buying your dream home, particularly if this is your first home. Think of it as one step toward that dream home, and listen to your Realtor's advice about which homes will have better resale value in the future. As I mentioned, many of my clients have traded up to better homes, often several times.

Recently, in fact, a past client approached me. When this couple bought a home, they swore they would live in the home for ten or more years. This was exactly where they wanted to be. It was less than two years later, and they wanted me to list their home for sale. But they had second thoughts because they said it would cost them an extra thousand dollars to sell their home. They reminded me that when they bought, I said, "I'll bet you a thousand dollars that you will not be in this home five years from now. In fact, you will probably move on in less than three years." I'd forgotten that bet and, of course, they hadn't taken me up on the bet, anyway; but it illustrates how people's needs and desires change over time.

There is no way to learn everything about a home before you buy it. You can learn a lot, and I will discuss some of those things here. But the neighborhood, your close neighbors, future plans by the community, are all factors you will discover over time. Your local government may decide to build a highway a few blocks away. Private enterprise may decide to put in a shopping center. Your job situation may change. Or you may simply decide that you would prefer living in another area for any of a variety of reasons. Very little in this life is permanent. So, while you may be perfectly happy with the home you choose to buy, do not be afraid to buy if everything is not perfect.

The key is to start. When you make the change from being a renter to being a homeowner, you will change your life. It is amazing the change in attitude people experience when they actually own the ground they live on. It is the same with businesses. I recently helped a business owner, who leased the building and land for his business, to purchase the real estate. His restaurant always required more of him than he liked. But recently, when I stopped in for a meal, he came over to tell me he'd spent the better part of the day repairing plumbing problems, and he was happy about it. "You know," he said, "before I owned this, I would have raised Cain with the landlord and I would have had to pay for the repair anyway, and it would have caused me grief for some time. Now, though it wasn't pleasant working with plumbing pipes, I knew it was my property, and I wanted to see what I could do. Now, it's fixed and I'm happy."

11. Negotiating the Deal

We just wanted to express our gratitude for all of the work you did in helping us with our many real estate transactions since arriving here. With the purchase of three properties and sales of two in four years (does that set some kind of a record?), each presented its own challenges. You helped us to obtain our first loan with a quick solution to what seemed an impossible obstacle. You went "all out" to sell our second property with at least five different marketing approaches. And ultimately orchestrated a smooth closing (with about 3 minutes to spare) on our current home that was almost rescheduled due to new construction delays. Thank you again. We couldn't have done it without you.

—Janelle and Eric Stremel

So you've decided on the right house and you are ready to make an offer. One piece of advice here is to avoid becoming too attached to the property yet. What I mean is, it's nice that you have found a home you feel you will be happy in, but you need to be willing to walk away if you can't make the right deal for it. With all the buyers I have worked with through the years, the only ones for whom I could not get any seller concessions were those few who fell in love with the home and the seller would not budge. They were willing to take the home at almost any price. In fact, this piece of real estate had already changed in their minds from simply being a house to being their home.

Assessing Your Position

If you haven't already done it, you and your Realtor® should now prepare for negotiation by formulating a game plan. You should both be clear about what things are vital to have included in the deal and what things you can give up. Most offers should include some unnecessary things you can give up without feeling deprived, while giving the sellers the sense that they got a concession from you. It is also important to understand that there are many more things to negotiate for than price. In fact, there are times when price is the least important negotiating objective. And yet, price is the one thing that nearly every buyer addresses.

If, for example, you do not have stellar credit and are unable to obtain conventional financing, you might want the seller to finance for you. In that case, do you really think the sellers, if they will provide financing, will also drop their price? Not normally. Or, you may need a really quick close—you will be homeless in two weeks, and have to be in your new home. If the new home is empty, you do not have a problem. But, if it means convincing the sellers to move out quickly, you may have to concede to the asking price in order to get what you need. On the other hand, you might want new carpet in the deal (and ask for it) but could live with the carpet that is in the home now. It is important to know and to clearly communicate to your agent those things which are important to you, and those which are not.

Always try to negotiate from a position of strength. You can contribute to a stronger negotiating position by getting pre-qualified or pre-approved for your home mortgage. It will also help if you are making an offer on a home that is clearly within your affordable limits. And if you have a home that must be sold first, it will help

73

greatly if you already have a contract by another buyer to purchase that home.

When you and your Realtor® have a clear picture of your negotiating position, you can move on to the next step.

Your Realtor® will also try to find out what might motivate the sellers. While it is not always possible to determine their motivations up front, it is usually worth trying. If, for example, you can find out that the sellers are having a new home built, and would prefer not to move out of their present home until the new one is ready, you can address that in an offer. If you are not in a hurry to move, and you can make a closing date or possession date agreeable to the sellers, don't you think they might be willing to negotiate on price?

If appliances are not included in the listing, it is usually because the sellers want to keep them. Your offer should include transferring them to you, even if you do not want them. You could then easily give them up, and may get another concession important to you in exchange.

If you can find out that the sellers are being transferred and need to move quickly, or are getting divorced, or are facing foreclosure, you will have accumulated information that is important to the negotiating process.

Once you know as much as you can about the sellers' position, you have one last step before preparing the offer.

Determining the Home Value

Before preparing an offer, you should know whether the asking price for the home is above, at, or below market value. This is done by your Realtor® preparing either a formal, or informal market analysis. By identifying other similar properties which have sold recently, determining the sales prices, and determining how those properties differ from the one you are considering, the two of you can readily see if you are starting from a position where you (1) accept the listing price as market value; (2) have to convince the sellers that their home is overpriced; (3) need to move quickly with a close-to-full-price offer to get a home priced below market.

In my experience, most homes are priced at or close to market value when a Realtor® is involved. Homes being sold directly by owners are typically over-priced. Usually, such sellers not only want to save the Realtor® commissions, but are also either unaware of what true market value is or are trying to push the market themselves. It's why 9 out of 10 properties that start out for-sale-by-owner end up listed by a Realtor®.

A home may be overpriced for many reasons. Often, it is just a "trial balloon," where the sellers just want to see if they can attract a better-than-normal offer. There are also Realtors® who "buy" listings. That is, against their own better judgment, they will agree to list a house over market in order to get the listing. These Realtors® may be desperate for business and afraid that they will lose the listing to their competition, or have been unable to present a convincing argument to the sellers to price their home appropriately.

There are sellers who simply insist that their home is worth more than any objective market analysis will indicate. For example, a home which was for-sale-by-owner for months, was overpriced, and now is listed with a Realtor®, may be priced even higher than it was prior to Realtor® representation. That is because the sellers insisted they wanted their net price, so they added Realtor® commissions to the price when they listed the home. This ends up being a collusion between two people, the homeowner and the Realtor®, both of whom are either desperate or greedy and unwilling to face reality. Homes like this usually stay on the market the longest and end up being sold for less than market value.

In the case of an overpriced home, it may be necessary for your Realtor® to include a market analysis with the offer when it is presented.

Homes may also be under-priced for the market. This generally occurs because sellers need to sell fast, or because their Realtor® doesn't have a firm grasp on market value. Sometimes, a Realtor® may convince a seller that market value is actually lower because the Realtor® wants a quick sale. When you find a property like this, and you determine that it is the property you want, do not take a hard negotiating position. Take your Realtor's advice, recognize that the property will be sold fast, and offer accordingly. In the past year, I have sold four properties where my buyer was the first, and the only, buyer to have seen the property. I check every day for new listings, and when one comes up that fits, I call my buyer immediately to see the property. These were cases where, over time, my buyers could not find the right property, the new listing was under-priced, and it fit my buyers perfectly. Even with full priced offers, they got bargains. Remember—**my buyers** got the homes, not someone else.

Negotiating on Price

In general terms, there are two primary approaches to negotiating a deal where price alone is the major consideration. One is to start low and know that you will probably reach an agreed-on price somewhere between your initial offer and the asking price. In fact, one of your Realtor's jobs here is to try to determine the bottom line for the seller. The second approach is to make a "take it or leave it" offer. I will generally try this when I have found a home priced above my buyer's ability to pay. If I feel that any offer my buyer can make would be lower than what I could negotiate normally, I take the attitude that there is nothing to lose by making the offer. So, together, my buyer and I establish the maximum offering price, make the offer there, and inform the listing agent that it is a "take it or leave it" offer. My buyers will not entertain a counter proposal except for "cosmetic" items—like the closing date or what is included in the sale. Believe it or not, I have had a number of deals accepted on that basis. When my buyer was well qualified at the offering price, offered a quick sale, and the seller was motivated for other reasons, it has worked—and my buyers got properties priced under market.

In most cases, however, you and your Realtor® will discuss a starting point at which to make an offer, expecting it to be countered. The idea is to find that point where the seller will sell and you will buy, where each feels he is getting a fair deal, and no one is being taken advantage of.

This is an important point: The vast majority of real estate deals, when both sides are represented, should come down to what is fair. It should end up being a win/win situation, where everyone feels satisfied with the deal. We have all dealt with buyers who "want a deal" and who are unwilling to pay fair market value for any property. They want to steal it, to stick a knife in the seller's back and then twist it when it's in. They are only looking for someone who is vulnerable, who has to sell at any price. I usually send buyers like this away.

Now, it is true that some deals are made like this. I have found properties on the verge of foreclosure, or where the seller has to make a quick sale to save himself from bankruptcy, and I have not hesitated to get one of my buyers into such a deal. But to take the attitude that you can only be happy if you have "screwed" the seller is, in my opinion, to corrupt the whole process of real estate sales.

At this time, the country in general is in a seller's market. The economy is growing and healthy, interest rates are low, and people generally have more disposable income. The market is very competitive—buyers starting out, moving up and investing. All of these factors contribute to appreciating values. Sellers and buyers know this and know that a home will, generally speaking, be sold for more today than it would have sold for a year ago. Remember, too, that there are sellers who are trying to "push" the market to get more than their home is worth, and there are Realtors® who will "buy" a listing by telling the seller he can get the price the seller wants. So, again, it is important to have chosen a good agent, one who will automatically show you property listings comparable to the one you are interested in which sold recently, and who can tell you if a particular property is overpriced or, as occasionally happens, under-priced.

Remember that when something is under-priced, and the home fits your needs, you need to act quickly. Make sure your Realtor® checks new listings every day, and you may be the next buyer who is the only one to see the property. It only takes quick, smart action, and you could own that bargain.

But it is also not unusual, in a hot market, for buyers to lose one, two, or more properties before they get realistic about their offers. It is not smart to make a low offer when your Realtor® has determined that the showing activity has been brisk, or that competing offers are either in or coming in. Listing Realtors® will often use the ploy of a competing offer to get you to raise your offer. So, you cannot always believe it. A property can sit on the market for an extended period of time with no offers, then have two or more submitted about the same time. I've seen it happen often enough, even on properties I have listed, to know that it is not all a conspiracy. So, again, it is important to have a feel for the market, to know the relative market value of the home you want to purchase, and to make an offer which is reasonable to the market.

The Offering Process

Once you and your Realtor® have done your research, he will prepare the actual offer (called a purchase contract, or a contract to buy and sell property), you will sign it, write a check for the earnest money, and it will be submitted to the seller or listing broker. See an example of such a contract in Appendix B. A note about earnest money: This is the money which accompanies the offer and signifies that you are entering this contract in good faith. You are putting that money at risk, although not at significant risk. It represents your agreement that you are serious about buying the home, that you will perform as promised under the offer, and that you will come to closing with the balance of the money needed to close the purchase on the home. Some Realtors® place a great deal of importance on the amount of earnest money presented with the offer, and feel that the more earnest money presented, the better the buyer is.

In the best of worlds, if you have enough money, and qualification is not a problem, submitting more earnest money will enhance your negotiating position. If you are a first-time home-buyer, and you are getting a low-down-payment or nothing-down loan, or you are borrowing the money from your parents, you may not have much, or any, earnest money to submit with the offer. I have submitted offers for first-time home-buyers with a promissory note as the earnest money, where the buyer promises to bring the money to closing (usually out of loan proceeds). I have also submitted offers with minimal earnest money (usually 1% of the purchase price is about the least acceptable). It is then incumbent on your Realtor® to attempt to convince the listing agent and the seller that the minimal earnest money is not a deterrent to your ability to purchase the home.

Your agent, in line with the research you have conducted together, will include one or more "extra" clauses in the contract which will establish agreements between you and the seller and/or ask for things you would like to have. For example, you might want to have the carpet professionally steam cleaned prior to closing. A paragraph in the contract could ask for that. If purchasing land on which to build a home, you would probably want to know if a survey, soil tests or other information is available, and to get that information by a certain date so that you can review it. A clause would be inserted to cover that need. There are so many clauses, and so many needs, that to cover them all would be impossible. You might review the sampling in Appendix C to see if any of them would work for you.

Once your offer is submitted to the sellers, there are three possible responses: (1) The seller accepts the offer as submitted, signs it, and you are under contract; (2) The seller counters your offer with another (called a counter proposal); or (3) the seller refuses to respond.

When the seller accepts your offer without question, do not try to second-guess the process. It is not time to worry that you offered too much or gave up too much. If you've done your homework, and you got what you wanted in the deal, be happy. The seller probably has an agent smart enough to advise them that the offer meets the seller's needs and it was not worthwhile trying to squeeze more out of it.

It is absolutely silly, however, for a seller to refuse to respond to a legitimate offer. I will not let one of my sellers ignore an offer. Recently, one of my sellers had a property on the market at $179,000, and an offer came in at $163,000. Her response was that the offer was an insult, and she would not even respond (this from a woman who regularly made very low offers on properties when she was the buyer). I told her that was not an option, that she hired me to sell her property, and part of my responsibility was to ensure that I communicate with every potential buyer until they have either bought the property or went away. She said, "Fine. Then tell them I'm holding out for full price." Which I did. Within an hour, the same buyer submitted a new offer at $176,000, and my seller accepted. There are, however, Realtors® who forget their objectivity, become emotionally involved and take offers personally. I've had listing Realtors®, when reviewing my buyer's low offer, tell me, with all the resentment they can muster, "This is an insult. My seller won't even respond to this." And I find myself having to remind that agent that he is not the seller, that I have a viable buyer who wants the property and is capable of buying it, and that if he insists on presenting the offer with the attitude he is displaying, he will run the risk of losing a sale for his seller.

Finally, most offers will elicit a counter proposal from the sellers. The negotiating process continues until you and the sellers have come to agreement on the price, terms, inclusions and exclusions which work for both of you. If both Realtors® and their clients have done their work responsibly, it should be a deal that makes everyone satisfied, even happy. It will be a win/win for everyone. When everyone has signed on the final counter proposal or redraft of the offer, you and the seller are "under contract." Your earnest money is deposited in an escrow account, and held until all the terms of your offer are met and the closing is held. While this process varies from state to state, in Colorado, the closing occurs as of a certain date with buyers, sellers, their agents, a lender and a title person all signing the appropriate closing documents. Prior to that time, however, there is work to be done.

12. Inspections, Title Documents and Other Contingencies

It was a bit unsettling when we retired and decided to move here from Ohio. We found the home we wanted during a trip made explicitly for the home search, and we knew there would be a lot to do after we returned to Ohio, not the least of which involved selling our home there. Fortunately, you were trustworthy, diligent, and kept us informed all the way, from coordinating home inspections, title documents, and even working with our lender. You even replaced our furnace filter! Our home was ready when we arrived, and the move-in was as painless as can be expected. It seems to us that things would have been far more precarious and stressful had we not hired you as our buyer's agent.

—Paul and Cora Winters

The offer you made to purchase property, once signed and agreed to by both you and the seller(s), becomes a contract. A contract is simply an agreement between two or more people (called parties) to do certain things, and in exchange, some form of compensation is paid. In this case, when you do what you have agreed to do in the contract, you get the house. When the sellers do the things they agreed to, they get the money.

Some of the responsibilities of the sellers are:

- Providing you with a property disclosure, which is the seller's best representation of the condition of the property and all the fixtures that will be sold to the buyer;

- Letting you know if there are any material defects about the property (required by most state laws);

- Providing you with a title commitment or an abstract of title;

- Providing you with declarations and bylaws or covenants and restrictions, documents which pertain to any homeowner's association or neighborhood group which might have some say as to what you can and cannot do with your home;

- Letting you and certain other people have access to the home for purposes of conducting a home inspection, an appraisal, taking measurements, etc.;

- Answering your legitimate questions about the house;

- Showing up at the appointed time to sign the documents to transfer title of the property to you.

Some of the responsibilities of the buyers are:

- Applying for a mortgage loan and providing all the information required by your lender to process that loan;

- Getting the money necessary to close the purchase—down payment and closing costs;

- Having an appraisal done (usually at your expense) to determine the current market value of the property;

- Conducting an inspection of the property, usually with the help of a professional home inspector;

- Reviewing the title and other documents provided to you by the sellers and determining if they are acceptable to you;

- Showing up at the appointed time to take title to the property and pay the sellers.

Nearly every contract has contingencies which give one party or the other the right to cancel the contract if certain things about the property are not satisfactory to that party, or certain obligations of the other party are not met. For example, the loan contingency clause requires the buyer to apply for a mortgage by a certain date, and to get loan approval by another certain date. If the buyer's lender anticipates problems getting loan approval it will be up to the buyers to cancel the contract by the loan approval deadline. In that event the property will be back on the market. The buyer has the right to review the title and association documents, and by a certain date, if the buyer finds those documents unacceptable, he can cancel the contract and go buy another property. Let's look at some of the major contingencies included in nearly every home purchase contract.

The Home Inspection

You normally have the right to conduct an inspection of the home you are purchasing to determine the condition of the home and all the things included in it. This contingency gives you the right to ask the sellers to remedy things which may reduce the value of the home, and to terminate the contract if you can't reach agreement with the seller on payment for these repairs.

If you are buying a condominium in a newer project, you may feel comfortable conducting the home inspection yourself. Some of my buyers have plugged a hair dryer into all the electrical outlets to make sure they were working, run the dishwasher, turned on all the burners on the stove, tried the oven, run water in all sinks, baths and toilets to make sure there were no leaks, and checked for other details which could be inspected by observation. Others have used professional home inspectors, particularly on older properties. You and your Realtor® should determine by a review of the condominium documents what things are the responsibility of the homeowner's association. For example, if heat is included in your dues, the association is generally responsible for maintaining heating systems. It is also generally responsible for outside maintenance, including painting, roof replacement, maintenance of common facilities such as a pool or clubhouse, and so on. But if the heating system is separate for each condominium, and the individual homeowners are responsible, then you must also inspect the heating system. In that case, you might need a professional.

If you are buying a home that is new construction (it's being built for you, or you put it under contract before it is completed), the purchase contract is probably full of clauses specially drafted by the seller to protect the seller. The state-approved sales contract forms do not address new construction, and many of the contracts are unconscionably oriented toward the seller. The best advice I can give to a buyer of new construction is (1) deal with a builder with a proven track record; (2) review the purchase contract carefully with your buyer agent; and (3) have your lawyer review the contract.

You generally, but not always, have the right to meet with the contractor shortly before closing on the purchase to inspect the construction. At this time, you will compile what is called a "punch list." This is a list of things you note that the builder must remedy within a period of time described in your contract. It may include nicks in the wall, broken tiles, doors that do not close properly, and anything else you can identify that needs fixing. The builder will usually have those repairs done after you move in, but within a time period such as thirty days. With new construction, you also have a builder's warranty, usually one year, during which time, the builder must fix anything that goes wrong due to faulty construction or materials. You will also have the warranties to appliances and other systems (such as furnaces) included in the house.

There is no automatic right to either a warranty or a pre-closing punchlist. Even though they are common, a buyer should carefully check the purchase contract for specifics. Some aggressive sellers, for example, require the buyer to waive all implied warranties in return for a short-term express warranty; this means that if the roof collapses after expiration of the express warranty period, the builder may refuse to repair. Other aggressive sellers of new construction require the buyer to close on the purchase before the home is ready for occupancy. A certificate of occupancy doesn't necessarily mean that the new home is clean, painted, landscaped, or that the stickers have been removed from the new windows. Again, read the contract with your agent carefully for details on these points.

If you are buying a used home (called a resale), it is important that, unless you are particularly well qualified, you hire a professional home inspector to do the inspection for you. I have even sold homes to general contractors who have hired home inspectors, because they realized that, even though they know a lot about homes, they do not know all the details of electrical, heating, plumbing or other systems in the homes. Your Realtor® should have a list of qualified home inspectors in the area and be able to recommend some good ones. Since home inspectors are not licensed in Colorado, anyone who wants to can be one. Therefore, I will only put inspectors on my recommended list who are bonded or insured, are members of a certifying organization such as the American Society of Home Inspectors, and whose competence I have observed during the inspection process.

A good home inspector has been trained in all the systems, all the details, which make up a house. A good home inspection will take from a couple of hours to a full day, depending on the size and complexity of the house. You should get a complete written report after the inspection is completed. You should always accompany your home inspector while he is going through the house. Even if the inspector finds nothing wrong with the home, you will learn a lot. Inspectors are great at giving tips on many things, for example, how to clean a dishwasher that has a build-up of hard water deposits (use Tang for one or two wash cycles—empty, of course). You will generally learn such things as how to change a furnace filter and how often to do so, along with other maintenance functions which will help you keep your home in good shape during your ownership.

At the completion of the inspection, the inspector may take you through the home just to emphasize what he observed that might need attention. Those are the things you want to discuss with your Realtor®. You may want to ask the sellers to remedy some or all of those items. It's also important to remember, when buying a resale home, that it is not going to be, nor is it meant to be, perfect. You should not "sweat the small stuff." For example, if all you find in the home inspection is that a bath tub or two needs caulking, or furnace filters need changing, or an outside door needs a new weather seal, or other minor details, you might agree that you could do the repairs yourself or have a maintenance man do them after you move in. However, occasionally the inspector will discover a condition that requires a specialist. For example, he may find a cracked foundation wall that may lead him to suspect that it is more than normal settling. In that case, he might recommend that you have a structural engineer inspect the foundation. Other serious items may require other specialists.

If anything major is discovered, however, it would be appropriate to request that the seller correct the situation. If the heat exchanger on the furnace has a leak, it needs to be replaced, and that can be a costly item. If any appliance does not work, you may ask that it be repaired or replaced. If the roof is in such disrepair, or so old, that replacement is imminent, you may ask the seller to have the roof replaced.

When you make your request to the sellers, the sellers may respond in a variety of ways. They may say, yes, they will have the items remedied prior to closing. They may say, no, that the price you negotiated on the house does not leave them the money to make the corrections. Or they may offer to settle with you somewhere in between. If they do not have the cash to fix the furnace, for example, but recognize that it needs repair, they may offer to compensate you at closing and let you have it repaired after the home is yours. As long as you and the seller can resolve the inspection items to the satisfaction of both of you, and you put the agreement in writing, you can proceed to closing. If you cannot resolve the issues, you have the opportunity to cancel the contract and move on. In fact, if you find that there is a serious, ongoing problem (like the foundation wall), you may want to terminate the contract outright. Under currently approved contracts, in fact, you may terminate the contract for no specific reason at all.

There is one other reason to have a professional home inspection. If you do not, and you discover problems with the home after your purchase, you may have given up your right to make a claim against the seller for those problems. It will depend on the legal issues involved, but almost no one wants to hire an attorney after the fact and spend hundreds or thousands of dollars when the small cost of an inspector would have provided the information you needed in advance. Assuming you have resolved the inspection issues, let's move on to title issues.

Title Documents

The contract will describe certain documents that the seller is obligated to provide to you, which are either in the form of a title commitment or an abstract of title. Whichever form it takes, it is a legal picture of the title to the property. It shows you who owns it (hopefully, the seller), the existing mortgage company and the initial amount of his loan, and other things about the property which need to be cleared up prior to closing or which might impede your ability to purchase the home.

You and your Realtor® should review these documents to ensure that there are no title problems that would prevent you from getting clear title to the property. For example, if there are liens or obligations against the property that total more than the purchase price, you would want to immediately inquire as to how those debts are going to be paid. Typically, you do not want to take title to a property that has obligations against it that cannot be cleared by the title company at closing. It might be that some of the obligations shown in the title documents have actually been paid, but the payments have not been recorded with the county clerk. A simple recording of those documents would clear those debts from the record.

Some problems that might be disclosed in a title search are very simple to remedy. For example, if title is shown to be held in the names of a husband and wife as joint tenants, and one of those persons has died, a simple recording of the death certificate will take that person off the title, thereby enabling the surviving spouse to transfer title to you.

Easements

You will also find things on virtually every set of title documents that will remain with the property even after sale. Utility companies which have power, sewer, water and cable lines running to the property will generally have a continuing easement to go onto your land (only in areas designated on the plat, which is a surveyor's exact drawing of the homesite) for purposes of repair, replacement or installation of their utilities. An easement is not actual title to, or ownership, of property. It is simply a recorded agreement giving access to another person or entity for limited purposes. Local governments might have easements for a variety of reasons. In the mountain towns of Colorado, governments often ask for and receive easements (at the time a subdivision is platted) giving them a place to dump snow off the roadway. The property you are considering may have an easement giving your neighbor the right to drive across your property to get to their home. Sometimes it is a shared driveway. Sometimes, they are unable to get reasonable access to their home in any other way. Or, you may have an easement across a neighbor's land.

A buyer should carefully review every easement that is shown by his title commitment to make sure it will not interfere with his enjoyment of the property.

Neighborhood and Condo Associations

Years ago (20, 30, 40 years or more), there was not a lot of community planning as neighborhoods were established and communities grew. That is why you can go to old neighborhoods and find that the types of homes are very different from each other (in the mountains, you often have "A-frame" homes next to mansions), and commercial and residential and industrial components can be randomly interspersed. Over time, governing authorities (town councils and county governments) have usually developed rules and regulations which give them the authority to approve what is built, to ensure that some consistency exists in each neighborhood development, and to designate how homes, stores, and industrial development will be separated.

Restrictions on building, both from governments and from developers, have flourished in the past 30 years, but for different reasons. Governments want to control growth and developers want to preserve values.

Therefore, depending on the neighborhood, there may be a set of documents filed with the governing authority by the developer which establish certain guidelines for that neighborhood. These are generally called the covenants, conditions and restrictions (CC&Rs) for that neighborhood. Often, these documents will incorporate a set of architectural guidelines which may be more or less restrictive.

If you are buying a condominium or townhouse, the documents are called the declaration and bylaws. And because these types of property are typically managed by a homeowners' association, there will also be a set of rules and regulations. The association collects dues, the amount of which it sets from time to time, and will have a set of financial documents showing how well it has managed the condominium complex.

All of these documents should be provided to you along with the title documents. If they are not, have your Realtor® determine if such documents exist, and if so, get copies for you. It is important that you review them. The restrictions imposed by these documents may be per-

fectly acceptable to you. For example, some neighborhood associations will not allow anyone to have junk
cars parked in front of homes and will not allow you to
conduct auto repairs on the property. The restrictions
were designed to ensure that only certain types of people
would live in the neighborhood—those who like the
restrictions. If you happen to be a backyard mechanic,
this may not work for you.

Some associations restrict the number of household
pets. Some condominium associations insist that anything stored on your deck (like bicycles) not be visible
from the street. All of these restrictions and requirements
should be reviewed by the buyer during the title review
period. An RV owner, for example, would be very unpleas-
antly surprised if he learned, after closing, that the covenants prohibited RVs from being parked anywhere on
the property.

When purchasing a condominium, townhouse or
other property that requires the payment of dues and
assessments, you should ask for and review the financial
statements of the association. You may also get copies of
the minutes of the past two or three meetings. These will
help you determine if the association is financially
viable—if it has established reserves to cover major peri-
odic maintenance such as roofs or paved parking areas
and painting. If reserves are not substantial enough,
homeowners could be faced with future special assessments. That is, every homeowner is asked to pay a set
amount (sometimes amounting to thousands of dollars)
to pay for a needed improvement to the complex as a
whole. A review of minutes, or a telephone call to a
member of the association board of directors can also get
you information about what the association is planning.

These are all things that should be disclosed to you in
the title documents. You will have an opportunity to
review these documents, and it is important that you do
so before the deadline for objection. If there is anything

you cannot live with, you will have the right to terminate your contract to purchase the home based on that review. If everything is in order, or at least within your limits of tolerance, then you can move on.

The Appraisal

If you are not paying cash for your property—that is, you are having part of the purchase financed with a mortgage loan—then the loan will generally be contingent on a satisfactory appraisal of value. You have the option of including an appraisal contingency if you are paying cash, but it will be required by the lender if you are financing. Appraisal is a process whereby an appraiser looks at the property you are purchasing, looks at similar properties that have been sold recently, and gives an opinion of the fair market value of your property. However, the appraiser also looks at the contract in place between you and the sellers. If he determines that the contract is at a price that is fairly close to the value established by looking at comparable sold properties, he will most likely establish a fair market value at or close to your contract price.

If your contract price is substantially different, then he may establish a fair market value either higher than or lower than your contract price. If the appraisal comes in at a value higher than what you have agreed to pay for the home, you can pat yourself on the back, for you and your Realtor® have negotiated a very good deal. If it comes in lower (even by $1), *and* you have made the appraisal a contingency in your contract, you have the right to terminate the contract. The contract can be kept intact, however, by one of three agreements: (1) You agree to pay a larger down payment (because your lender will only lend based on the appraised value); (2) The sellers agree to lower the contract price; or (3) you and the sellers agree to settle someplace in between.

If the appraisal does come in low and you have an appropriate appraisal contingency in your contract, you may have the opportunity to turn away from this deal and go find another home, or to negotiate further with the sellers. Again, you have the chance to decide.

Financing

If you are financing your purchase, there will be a contingency for that. In other words, you are given a certain amount of time for your lender to approve a loan for you within certain established parameters. You may put in the contract that you want a 95% loan with an interest rate no more than 7.5%, with payments over 30 years. In Colorado, if by the loan approval deadline, you do not have full loan approval at terms acceptable to you, you must provide written notice to the sellers to terminate the contract. If you are having some difficulty getting the loan you want, and a lender suggests another loan that will work, you and your Realtor® may want to try to negotiate an extension of the contract and establish new loan terms based on the new loan. Whether the sellers agree to cooperate will depend on how interested they are in continuing to work with you. If you do not terminate the contract under the loan contingency, and subsequently, you fail to qualify for your loan and cannot purchase the home, you will be considered in default. In Colorado, this means that, at a minimum, you will lose the earnest money you paid. It is critically important that both you and your Realtor® be cognizant on all contract deadlines and do what is necessary to perform your obligations by those deadlines. Then you will be able to protect your rights under the contract, including your right to terminate, if necessary.

Other Contingencies

Other contingencies can also be built into an offer, the inclusion of which will depend on a variety of circumstances. For example, if you must sell your current home before you will have the money to purchase the new home, and you cannot wait to put the new home under contract, you will need a contingency stating that if you cannot sell your existing home, you can terminate the contract on the new home. Usually, if a seller accepts this contingency, he will want to put a definite time limit on it.

If you are buying raw land, and have plans to build a home or other building, you will want time to determine what exactly you can build and, possibly, to meet with planning commissions and other governing authorities to determine if you can build what you want. You may also want to research other aspects of the land. For instance, has toxic waste ever been disposed of on the land? Can you get access? Is it served by an established infrastructure (like water, sewer, gas and electricity), or will you have to establish your own? Do others have rights to use the land? Can you get the financing you need to build? If you are using the Colorado State-approved purchase contract, and you want to accomplish the research necessary, your Realtor® should include what is called a "due diligence" contingency. This contingency states that you have a defined time period to conduct any and all research on the land that you see fit, and if, for any reason, you find the land unacceptable, you can terminate the contract. Under the Colorado contract, this contingency is clearly covered in the inspection provision.

If there are special problems with the property, you may want to engage the sellers' efforts to have those problems removed and make your offer contingent on the successful accomplishment of that action. For instance, if a neighbor has an outbuilding or driveway that encroaches on the property you want, you may ask that the sellers take the steps necessary to eliminate the encroachment. You clearly do not want to inherit a problem, and since the sellers presumably have an established relationship with their neighbors, it might be relatively easy for them to get this accomplished. Often, conditions like this may not be discovered until you receive and review the title documents. And, while title documents address these issues in general, you may, at this time, want to amend the contract to specifically address those things you want resolved as a condition of going forward.

There may be other contingencies that make sense to incorporate into your contract or an amendment to it, and all the relevant circumstances should be discussed with your Realtor®. Be careful not to incorporate frivolous contingencies, because they may make the contract unattractive to the seller. But intelligently drafted contingencies could mean the difference for you between disaster and success.

13. Getting to the Closing Table and Moving In

I am writing to express my appreciation for the manner in which you assisted me in my search for a home. I also wish to commend you for your efforts in the subsequent negotiations prior to the closing of the purchase. Thanks to you, the entire process went smoothly and was completed without a hitch or a hang-up. The thirty-minute closing, from the time we walked to the table until we walked out the door, must be some kind of record.

—Mark Kelley

B y now, you might be feeling as if you've completed a college course. Well, it's true. It gives you just some idea of what a Realtor® has to learn to navigate in this business. It seems easy because I do it every day. And, of course, most transactions are fairly normal, predictable events where the standard actions are taken, nothing out of the ordinary is discovered, no financing problems exist, title documents are clean, the inspection is uneventful, and everyone comes to the closing table happy. We have to always be prepared, however, for the worst.

I've covered lots of potential disasters in this book, but there are more. Real estate transactions, when complicated by whatever reason, tend to take on their own personality and character. Every Realtor® has experienced deals that fell apart and didn't close, sometimes at the last minute. When that happens, the people involved are usually pointing fingers, often blaming the nearest or most convenient target.

The Sale That Didn't Happen

One of my earliest transactions involved a single mother who was selling her home and buying another. The home Julie was selling was called a "cluster home"— that is, it was located in a home project governed by a homeowners' association. It was just like a townhouse or condominium project, except that the homes were all detached. Another Realtor® had produced a buyer, so we had her home under contract. In addition, we had found a home she wanted, and put it under contract for her. Everything was going smoothly, except that the lender for her buyers did not get loan approval on time. I talked with him every day, and he assured me that, even though this purchase was the maximum that the buyers could handle, loan approval was assured. Their credit was fine, the ratios were close but acceptable—but the underwriter was just overloaded. So we waited. And Julie and her kids packed—and scheduled a moving company.

On the day we were supposed to close on both the sale of Julie's old home and the purchase of her new home, with the house full of packed boxes, and the moving van parked outside, I got a call from the lender. The loan had been denied for the buyers. It seems the lender did not notice that there were homeowners' association dues involved with Julie's home and did not include that information in the loan package. Of course, he blamed me for not informing him of that fact. I simply referred him to the contract, in which that information was detailed (of course, the contract is one of the first loan documents available to the lender).

Well, it was a disaster. The number of people negatively affected was enough to cause a relatively new Realtor® to quit the business before any more people were hurt. The buyers' lease had ended, and they had to move out of their apartment, now with no place to go. Julie and her two children had to stay in their home and live out of boxes until I could get her home sold again. The sellers of the home that she was scheduled to buy wanted to keep her earnest money, they were so angry (but we had the sale of her home as a contingency, so she got her money back), and those sellers had to cancel their pending purchase of another new home. And, although not very important to all the parties involved, none of the Realtors® involved got paid. We all had to do our work over again.

I kept telling Julie through her tears that things happen for a reason in this world, and we would get her house sold and find her an even better home to move into. And that actually happened. When it was all said and done, she had a house far superior to the one she would have bought, in a nicer neighborhood, closer to the schools her children would attend, and she ended up happy. But what a process getting there! I wouldn't wish that to happen to anyone.

Therefore, we build in contingencies to contracts, and we try to cover all the bases so that everything that is promised actually occurs. For example, every contract should have a clause that lets you go into the home one or two days prior to closing to do a final walk-through. This lets you verify that, (a) the home is in at least as good a condition as it was when you put it under contract; and (b) that the sellers have done those things they promised. If your contract, for example, called for having the carpets professionally steam cleaned (note the language—you generally don't want to settle for the sellers renting a do-it-yourself cleaner), you can make sure that was done. If they were to have certain things repaired or replaced as a result of the inspection agreement, you can verify that they were completed.

Keep in mind, typically, there is nothing in the contract that obligates a seller to actually clean the house for you. Usually, it is common courtesy to do so, but if that is important to you, put it in the contract. You see, contracts simply keep everything nice and tidy. If everyone you dealt with were completely honest, had an impeccable memory, and always had it in his heart to do the right thing, contracts probably wouldn't be necessary. But even honest people have short memories, or get in a hurry, or decide they already gave too much. So we have contracts.

Do your walk-through with your Realtor®. Bring to the listing agent's attention anything that wasn't completed according to the contract, and have it corrected prior to closing. Ultimately, you hold the trump card. You have the money to hand over at the closing table, and if everything was not done as agreed, you can say, no, you're not going to close. Now, practically speaking, that rarely happens, and everything is in place to close. You probably have packed or otherwise made plans to move out of your current residence, you are excited about being in a new home, and the pressure is on everyone to go ahead and sign. So, again, I suggest that you don't sweat the small stuff.

Anything significant could be handled with a written agreement at closing, or by escrowing money. For example, let's say that the seller was to replace the furnace, but could not get a plumber in to complete that job in time. You could all agree that the title company would withhold the money for that from the proceeds due to the seller, and the title company would then pay the plumber when the work is complete. If the carpet was supposed to be cleaned, but wasn't, the seller could hand you a check at closing so you would have the money to pay for it.

And what do you do if the seller refuses? You have to decide. Is it more important to close, or should you walk away? I'm telling you this, not because it happens a lot, but because it does happen occasionally. And it's best to be prepared.

100

If your transaction is typical, everything will have been completed per agreement, you sign the closing papers, present your check, and get the keys to the house. And everybody walks away with big grins on their faces, looking forward to the new life they have created.

Now for the fun part. It's time to move in.

To Reach Ken Deshaies
Mail: P.O. Box 37
Dillon, CO 80435
Phone: (888) 668-9171
Fax: (970) 468-2758

To find out how to you can become a
published author, check out;
www.InstantAuthor.com
or e-mail renniecoach@earthlink.net

APPENDIX A

Sample Buyer-Agency Contract

(Colorado Approved Form)

APPENDIX A

Sample Buyer-Agency Contract

(Colorado Approved Form)

Appendix A

RE/MAX Properties of the Summit
131 Blue River Parkway, Silverthorne P.O. Drawer 2929, Dillon, CO 80435
Ken Deshaies Broker Associate

THIS FORM HAS IMPORTANT LEGAL CONSEQUENCES AND THE PARTIES SHOULD CONSULT LEGAL AND TAX OR OTHER COUNSEL BEFORE SIGNING.

Compensation charged by real estate brokers is not set by law. Such charges are established by each real estate broker.

DIFFERENT BROKERAGE RELATIONSHIPS ARE AVAILABLE WHICH INCLUDE BUYER AGENCY, SELLER AGENCY, SUBAGENCY TRANSACTION-BROKER.

EXCLUSIVE RIGHT-TO-BUY CONTRACT
(BUYER AGENCY)

_____, Colorado

<u>_____</u>
Name(s) of Buyer(s)

("Buyer") appoint **RE/MAX Properties of the Summit**
Broker's Name

("Broker") as Buyer's exclusive agent for the purpose of representing Buyer to acquire interests in real property as indicated in Section 3 ("Property") under the terms specified herein.

1. Effect of Exclusive Buyer Agency Contract. Broker is the limited agent of Buyer and will represent only Buyer.
By engaging Broker as Buyer's exclusive agent, Buyer agrees to conduct all negotiations for Property through Broker and to refer to Broker all inquiries received from real estate brokers, salespersons, prospective sellers, or any other source during the time this contract is in effect. Buyer agrees that compensation to Broker which is conditioned upon the acquisition by Buyer of interests in real property, whether by lease or purchase (collectively "Purchase"), will be earned by Broker whenever such interests are acquired by Buyer directly or indirectly, without any discount or allowance for efforts made by Buyer or any other person in connection with the acquisition of such interests by Buyer.

2. Purchase. "Purchase of the Property" or "Purchase" means the voluntary acquisition of any interest in the Property or the voluntary creation of a right to acquire any interest in the Property (including a contract or lease).

3. Property. The Property shall substantially meet the following requirements or be otherwise acceptable to Buyer:

4. Duration of Agency. Broker's authority as Buyer's exclusive agent shall begin _____, and shall continue until the earlier of _____, or completion of the acquisition of the Property.

5. Broker's Services. Broker will exercise reasonable skill and care for Buyer, and make reasonable efforts to locate property.
  (a) Broker will promote the interests of Buyer with the utmost good faith, loyalty, and fidelity, including but not limited to:
    (1) seeking a price and terms which are acceptable to Buyer, except that Broker shall not be obligated to seek other properties while Buyer is a party to a contract to purchase Property;
    (2) procuring acceptance of any offer to purchase property and to assist in the completion of the transaction;
    (3) presenting all offers to and from Buyer in a timely manner, regardless of whether Buyer is already a party to a contract to purchase Property;
    (4) disclosing to Buyer adverse material facts actually known to Broker;
    (5) counseling Buyer as to any material benefits or risks of the transaction which are actually known to Broker;
    (6) advising Buyer to obtain expert advice as to material matters about which Broker knows but the specifics of which are beyond the expertise of Broker;
    (7) accounting in a timely manner for all money and property received, and
    (8) informing Buyer that Buyer may be vicariously liable for the acts of Broker when Broker is acting within the scope of the agency relationship.
  (b) Broker shall <u>not</u> disclose to the seller or any other third party, without the informed consent of Buyer:
    (1) that Buyer is willing to pay more than the purchase price for Property;
    (2) what Buyer's motivating factor(s) are;
    (3) that Buyer will agree to financing terms other than those offered;

Forms by Exceed 98 Agent Automation (800) 757-3903 www.exceedsystems.com

Initials _____ _____ _____ _____   October 26, 1999 8:53:01 PM   Page: 1 of
The printed portions of this form, except the (*italicized*) (**differentiated**) insertions, have been approved by the Colorado Real Estate Commission. (BC 17-9-95)

104

Sample Buyer-Agency Contract

(4) any material information about Buyer unless disclosure is required by law or failure to disclose such information would constitute fraud or dishonest dealing; and

(5) any facts or suspicions regarding circumstances which would psychologically impact or stigmatize Property.

(c) Broker shall disclose to any prospective seller all adverse material facts actually known by Broker, including but not limited to adverse material facts concerning Buyer's financial ability to perform the terms of the transaction and whether Buyer intends to occupy Property as a principal residence.

(d) Broker shall make submissions to Buyer describing and identifying properties appearing to substantially meet the criteria set forth in Section 3.

6. Costs of Services or Products Obtained from Outside Sources. Broker will not obtain or order products or services from outside sources unless Buyer has agreed to pay for them promptly when due. (Examples: surveys, soil tests, radon tests, title reports, property inspections.)

7. Compensation to Broker. In consideration of the services to be performed by Broker, Buyer shall pay Broker as follows: [Instruction: If any of the forms of compensation set forth in subsections (b), (c), or (d) will not be used, write "N/A" in the blank(s) of such subsection(s).]

(a) **Success Fee.** Broker shall be paid a fee equal to the greater of $_____ or _____% of the purchase price. The success fee is conditioned upon the Purchase of the Property or the acquisition by Buyer of property not in compliance with the requirements specified in Section 3 but within the purview of this contract. This fee is payable upon closing of the transaction(s), subject to the provisions of Section 8. This fee shall apply to Property contracted for during the original term of this contract or any extension(s) and shall also apply to Property contracted for within _____ days after this contract expires or is terminated (Holdover Period) if the Property was shown or specifically presented in writing to Buyer by Broker during the original term or any extension(s) of the term of this contract; provided, however, that Buyer shall owe no commission to Broker under this subsection if a commission is earned by another licensed real estate broker acting pursuant to an exclusive right-to-buy contract or an exclusive agency listing contract entered into during the Holdover Period.

Buyer is obligated to pay Broker's fee. However, Broker is authorized and instructed to request payment of Broker's fee in any of the following indicated methods:

☐ BY LISTING BROKER.

☐ BY SELLER FROM THE TRANSACTION.

☐ OTHER

(b) **Hourly Fee.** Buyer shall pay to Broker at the rate of $_____ per hour for time spent by Broker pursuant to this contract, to be paid to Broker when billed to Buyer.

(c) **Retainer Fee.** Buyer shall pay Broker a nonrefundable retainer fee of $_____ due and payable upon signing of this contract
This amount ☐ shall ☐ shall not be credited against fees payable to Broker in this Section 7.

(d) **Other**

8. Failure to Close. If a seller fails to close with no fault on the part of Buyer, the success fee provided in Section 7(a) shall be waived. If Buyer is at fault, such success fee will not be waived, but will be due and payable immediately. Broker shall not be obligated to advance funds for Buyer.

9. Disclosure of Broker's Role. At the earliest reasonable opportunity, Broker shall inform any prospective sellers or their brokers with whom Broker negotiates pursuant to this contract that Broker is acting on behalf of a Buyer-principal.

10. Disclosure of Buyer's Identity. Broker ☐ does ☐ does not have Buyer's permission to disclose Buyer's identity to third parties without prior written consent of Buyer.

11. Dual Agency/Transaction-Broker. If a written Dual Agency or Transaction-Broker Addendum is signed by Buyer, Broker may show Buyer properties listed by Broker.

12. Other Buyers. Broker may show properties in which Buyer is interested to other prospective buyers without breaching any duty or obligation to Buyer.

13. Assignment by Buyer. No assignment of Buyer's rights or obligations under this contract and no assignment of rights or obligations in property obtained for Buyer under this contract shall operate to defeat any of Broker's rights.

14. Nondiscrimination. The parties agree not to discriminate unlawfully against any prospective seller because of the race, creed, color, sex, marital status, national origin, familial status, physical or mental handicap, religion or ancestry of such person.

15. Recommendation of Legal Counsel. By signing this document, Buyer acknowledges that Broker has advised that this document has important legal consequences and has recommended consultation with legal and tax or other counsel, before signing this contract.

16. Alternative Dispute Resolution: Mediation. If a dispute arises relating to this contract, and is not resolved, the parties involved in such dispute (Disputants) shall first proceed in good faith to submit the matter to mediation. The Disputants will jointly appoint an acceptable mediator and will share equally in the cost of such mediation. In the event the entire dispute is not resolved within thirty (30) calendar days from the date written notice requesting mediation is sent by one Disputant to the other(s), the mediation, unless otherwise agreed, shall terminate. This section shall not alter any date in this contract, unless otherwise agreed.

The printed portions of this form, except the (*italicized*) (**differentiated**) insertions, have been approved by the Colorado Real Estate Commission. (BC 17-9-95)

Appendix A

17. Attorney Fees. In case of arbitration or litigation between Buyer and Broker in their respective capacities, the parties agree that costs and reasonable attorney fees shall be awarded to the prevailing party.

18. Additional Provisions: (The language of these additional provisions has not been approved by the Colorado Real Estate Commission.)

19. Modification of this Contract. No subsequent modification of any of the terms of this contract shall be valid, binding upon the parties, enforceable unless in writing and signed by the parties.

20. Entire Agreement. This contract constitutes the entire agreement between the parties and any prior agreements, whether oral or written, have been merged and integrated into this contract.

21. Counterparts. If more than one person is named as a Buyer herein, this contract may be executed by each Buyer, individually, and when executed, such copies taken together shall be deemed to be a full and complete contract between the parties.

22. Copy of Contract. Buyer acknowledges receipt of a copy of this contract signed by Broker.

Accepted   :RE/MAX Properties of the Summit

By:_____

       Broker

Address: 131 Blue River Parkway, Silverthorne P.O. Drawer 2929, Dillon, CO 80435

Phone: 468-2000

_____

Buyer

_____

Buyer

Address:

Phone:

The printed portions of this form, except the (*italicized*) (**differentiated**) insertions, have been approved by the Colorado Real Estate Commission. (BC 17-9-95)

b. That Seller is willing to accept less than the asking price for the property;

c. What the motivating factors are for any party buying or selling the property;

d. That Seller or Buyer will agree to financing terms other than those offered;

e. Any material information about the other party unless either:

    (1) the disclosure is required by law,

    (2) the disclosure pertains to adverse material facts about Buyer's financial ability to perform the terms of the transaction,

    (3) the disclosure pertains to Buyer's intent to occupy the property as a principal residence, or

    (4) failure to disclose such information would constitute fraud or dishonest dealing.

5. **NO DUTY FOR TRANSACTION-BROKER TO INVESTIGATE.** Broker, when acting as a Transaction-Broker, has no duty to conduct an independent inspection of the property for the benefit of Buyer and has no duty to independently verify the accuracy or completeness of statements made by Seller or independent inspectors. Broker, when acting as a Transaction-Broker, has no duty to conduct an independent investigation of Buyer's financial condition or to verify the accuracy or completeness of any statement made by Buyer.

6. **ADDITIONAL PROVISIONS.**

Accepted:

_____   _____
Seller or Buyer   Date   Seller or Buyer   Date

Broker: RE/MAX Properties of the Summit   131 Blue River Parkway, Silverthorne P.O. Drawer 2929, Dillon, CO 80435

By: _____
    Ken Deshaies Broker Associate   Date

Forms by Exceed 98 Agent Automation (800) 757-3903 www.exceedsystems.com

Initials _____ _____ _____ _____   October 26, 1999 8:54:34 PM   Page: 2 of 2
The printed portions of this form, except the (*italicized*) (**differentiated**) insertions, have been approved by the Colorado Real Estate Commission. (TBA 29-9-99)

107

APPENDIX B

Sample Contract to Buy and Sell Real Estate

(Colorado Approved Form)

Appendix B

RE/MAX Properties of the Summit
131 Blue River Parkway, Silverthorne P.O. Drawer 2929, Dillon, CO 80435
Ken Deshaies Broker Associate

The printed portions of this form have been approved by the Colorado Real Estate Commission. (CBS 1-9-99)

**THIS FORM HAS IMPORTANT LEGAL CONSEQUENCES AND THE PARTIES SHOULD CONSULT
LEGAL AND TAX OR OTHER COUNSEL BEFORE SIGNING.**

CONTRACT TO BUY AND SELL REAL ESTATE
(RESIDENTIAL)

Date:

1.   **AGREEMENT.** Buyer agrees to buy and the undersigned Seller agrees to sell the Property defined below on the terms and conditions set forth in this contract.

2.   **DEFINED TERMS.**
   a.   **Buyer.** Buyer,_____ , will take title to the real property described below as
   ☐ **Joint Tenants**   ☐ **Tenants In Common**   ☐ **Other____.**
   b.   **Property.** The Property is the following legally described real estate:

in the County of _____, Colorado, commonly known as No.

Street Address   City   State   Zip

together with the interests, easements, rights, benefits, improvements and attached fixtures appurtenant thereto, all interest of Seller in vacated streets and alleys adjacent thereto, except as herein excluded.

   c.   **Dates and Deadlines.**

Item No.	Reference	Event	Date or Deadline
1	§ 5a	Loan Application Deadline	
2	§ 5b	Loan Commitment Deadline	
3	§ 5c	Buyer's Credit Information Deadline	
4	§ 5c	Disapproval of Buyer's Credit Deadline	
5	§ 5d	Existing Loan Documents Deadline	
6	§ 5d	Objection to Existing Loan Deadline	
7	§ 5d	Approval of Loan Transfer Deadline	
8	§ 6a	Appraisal Deadline	
9	§ 7a	Title Deadline	
10	§ 7a	Survey Deadline	
11	§ 7b	Document Request Deadline	
12	§ 7c, § 8a	Governing Documents & Title Objection Deadline	
13	§ 8b	Off-Record Matters Deadline	
14	§ 8b	Off-Record Matters Objection Deadline	
15	§ 8e	Right Of First Refusal Deadline	
16	§ 10	Seller's Property Disclosure Deadline	
17	§ 10a	Inspection Objection Deadline	
18	§ 10b	Resolution Deadline	
19	§ 11	**Closing Date**	
20	§ 16	Possession Date	
21	§ 16	Possession Time	

Forms by Exceed 98 Agent Automation (800) 757-3903 www.exceedsystems.com

Initials _____ _____ _____ _____   October 26, 1999 8:19:31 PM Page: 1 of 11
The printed portions of this form, except the (*italicized*) (**differentiated**) insertions, have been approved by the Colorado Estate Commission. (CBS 1-9-99)

22	§ 28	Acceptance Deadline Date	
23	§ 28	Acceptance Deadline Time	

28
29   **d.**   **Attachments.** The following exhibits, attachments and addenda are a part of this contract:
30   **e.**   **Applicability of Terms.** A check or similar mark in a box means that such provision is applicable. The
31 abbreviation "N/A" means not applicable.
32 **3.**   **INCLUSIONS AND EXCLUSIONS.**
33   **a.**   The Purchase Price includes the following items (Inclusions):
34   **(1)**   **Fixtures.**   If attached to the Property on the date of this contract, lighting, heating,
35 plumbing, ventilating, and air conditioning fixtures, TV antennas, inside telephone wiring and connecting blocks/jacks,
36 plants, mirrors, floor coverings, intercom systems, built-in kitchen appliances, sprinkler systems and controls, built-in
37 vacuum systems (including accessories), garage door openers including _____ remote controls; and
38   **(2)**   **Other Inclusions.**   If on the Property whether attached or not on the date of this
39 contract: storm windows, storm doors, window and porch shades, awnings, blinds, screens, window coverings, curtain
40 rods, drapery rods, fireplace inserts, fireplace screens, fireplace grates, heating stoves, storage sheds, and all keys. Check
41 applicable box(es) if included: ☐ **Water Softeners,**   ☐   **Smoke/Fire Detectors,**
42 ☐   **Security Systems,**   ☐   **Satellite Systems** (including satellite dishes and accessories); and
43   **(3)**   **Parking and Storage Facilities**. The use of the following parking facility(ies):_____; and the
44 following storage facilities: _____.
45   **(4)**   **Water Rights.** The following legally described water rights:
46
47   **b.**   **Instruments of Transfer**. The Inclusions are to be conveyed at Closing free and clear of all taxes, liens
48 and encumbrances, except as provided in § 12. Conveyance shall be by bill of sale or other applicable legal instrument(s).
49 Any water rights shall be conveyed by _____ deed or other applicable legal instrument(s).
50   **c.**   **Exclusions.**   The following attached fixtures are excluded from this sale: _____.
51
52 **4.**   **PURCHASE PRICE AND TERMS.** The Purchase Price set forth below shall be payable in U. S. Dollars by
53 Buyer as follows:
54

Item No.	Reference	Item	Amount	Amount
1	§ 4	Purchase Price	$	
2	§ 4a	Earnest Money		$
3	§ 4b	New Loan		$
4	§ 4c	Assumption Balance		$
5	§ 4d	Seller or Private Financing		$
6	§ 4e	Cash at Closing		$
7		**TOTAL**	$	$

55
56   **a.**   **Earnest Money.** The Earnest Money set forth in this Section, in the form of _____, is part payment of
57 the Purchase Price and shall be payable to and held by _____, in its trust account, on behalf of both Seller and Buyer.
58 The parties authorize delivery of the Earnest Money deposit to the Closing Company, if any, at or before Closing.
59   **b.**   **New Loan.** Buyer shall obtain a new loan set forth in this Section and as follows:
60 ☐ **Conventional**   ☐ **FHA**   ☐ **VA**   ☐ **Other**
61 This loan will be secured by a _____ (1st, 2nd, etc.) deed of trust.
62   The loan may be increased to add the cost of mortgage insurance, VA funding fee and other items for a total loan
63 amount, not in excess of $_____, which shall be amortized over a period of _____ years at approximately $
64 _ per month including principal and interest not to exceed _____% per annum, plus, if required by Buyer's lender, a
65 monthly deposit of 1/12 of the estimated annual real estate taxes, property insurance premium, and mortgage insurance

---

Forms by Exceed 98 Agent Automation (800) 757-3903   www.exceedsystems.com

Initials _____ _____ _____ _____   October 26, 1999 8:22:40 PM Page: 2 of 11
The printed portions of this form, except the (*italicized*) (**differentiated**) insertions, have been approved by the Colorado Real
Estate Commission. (CBS 1-9-99)

111

66   premium. If the loan is an adjustable interest rate or graduated payment loan, the monthly payments and interest rate
67   initially shall not exceed the figures set forth above.
68   Loan discount points, if any, shall be paid to lender at Closing and shall not exceed _____% of the total loan
69   amount. Notwithstanding the loan's interest rate, the first _____ loan discount points shall be paid by _____, and the
70   balance, if any, shall be paid by _____.
71   Buyer shall timely pay Buyer's loan costs and a loan origination fee not to exceed _____% of the loan amount.
72   **c.   Assumption.** Buyer agrees to assume and pay an existing loan in the approximate amount of the
73   Assumption Balance set forth in this Section, presently payable at $_____ per month including principal, interest
74   presently at _____% per annum, and also including escrow for the following as indicated:
75   ☐ **Real Estate Taxes,**   ☐ **Property Insurance Premium,**   ☐ **Mortgage Insurance Premium,** and _____.
76   Buyer agrees to pay a loan transfer fee not to exceed $_____. At the time of assumption, the new interest rate
77   shall not exceed _____% per annum and the new monthly payment shall not exceed $_____ principal and interest, plus
78   escrow, if any. If the actual principal balance of the existing loan at Closing is less than the Assumption Balance, which
79   causes the amount of cash required from Buyer at Closing to be increased by more than $ _____, then ☐ **Buyer May**
80   **Terminate** this contract effective upon receipt by Seller of Buyer's written notice of termination or ☐ _____.
81   Seller ☐ **Shall**   ☐ **Shall Not** be released from liability on said loan, and if a VA-guaranteed loan, Seller's
82   eligibility ☐ **Shall**   ☐ **Shall Not** be reinstated. If applicable, compliance with the requirements for release from
83   liability or reinstatement of eligibility shall be evidenced by delivery at Closing of appropriate letter of commitment from
84   ☐ **VA**   ☐ **Lender.** Cost payable for release of liability/reinstatement of VA eligibility shall be paid by _____ in an
85   amount not to exceed $_____.
86   **d.   Seller or Private Financing.** Buyer agrees to execute a promissory note payable to: _____, as   ☐
87   **Joint Tenants**   ☐ **Tenants in Common**   ☐ **Other** _____, on the note form as indicated:
88   ☐ **(UCCC - No Default Rate)** NTD 82-3-95   ☐ **(Default Rate)** NTD 81-11-83
89   ☐ **Other** _____ secured by a _____ (1st, 2nd, etc.) deed of trust encumbering the Property, using the form as indicated:
90   ☐ **Strict Due-On-Sale (TD 72-7-96)**   ☐ **Creditworthy (TD 73-7-96)**   ☐ **Assumable - Not Due On Sale (TD**
91   **74-7-96)**   ☐ **Other** _____.
92   Buyer ☐ **Shall**   ☐ **Shall Not** execute and deliver, at Closing, a Security Agreement and UCC-1 Financing
93   Statement granting the holder of the promissory note a _____ (1st, 2nd, etc.) lien on the personal property included in
94   this sale. The promissory note shall be amortized on the basis of _____ ☐ years ☐ months, payable at $_____ per
95   month including principal and interest at the rate of _____% per annum. Payments shall commence _____ and shall be
96   due on the _____ day of each succeeding month. If not sooner paid, the balance of principal and accrued interest shall be
97   due and _____ after Closing. Payments ☐ **Shall**   ☐ **Shall** Not be increased by 1/12 of estimated annual real estate
98   taxes, and ☐ **Shall**   ☐ **Shall Not** be increased by 1/12 of estimated annual property insurance premium. The loan
99   shall also contain the following terms: if any payment is not received within _____ calendar days after its due date, a late
100 charge of _____% of such monthly payment shall be due. Interest on lender disbursements under the deed of trust shall
101 be _____% per annum. Default interest rate shall be _____% per annum. Buyer may prepay without a penalty _____.
102   Buyer ☐ **Shall**   ☐ **Shall Not** provide a mortgagee's title insurance policy, at Buyer's expense.
103   **e.   Cash at Closing.** All amounts paid by Buyer at Closing including Cash at Closing, plus Buyer's closing
104 costs, shall be in funds which comply with all applicable Colorado laws, which include cash, electronic transfer funds,
105 certified check, savings and loan teller's check and cashier's check (Good Funds).
106 **5.   FINANCING CONDITIONS AND OBLIGATIONS.**
107   **a.   Loan Application.** If Buyer is to pay all or part of the Purchase Price by obtaining a new loan, or if an
108 existing loan is not to be released at Closing, Buyer, if required by such lender, shall make written application by **Loan**
109 **Application Deadline** (§ 2c). Buyer shall cooperate with Seller and lender to obtain loan approval, diligently and timely
110 pursue same in good faith, execute all documents and furnish all information and documents required by lender, and,
111 subject to § 4, timely pay the costs of obtaining such loan or assumption consent. Buyer agrees to satisfy the reasonable
112 requirements of lender, and shall not withdraw the loan or assumption application, nor intentionally cause any change in
113 circumstances which would prejudice lender's approval of the loan application or funding of the loan.
114   **b.   Loan Commitment.** If Buyer is to pay all or part of the Purchase Price by obtaining a new loan as
115 specified in § 4b, this contract is conditional upon Buyer obtaining a written loan commitment including, if required by
116 lender, (1) lender verification of employment, (2) lender approval of Buyer's credit-worthiness, (3) lender verification
117 that Buyer has sufficient funds to close, and (4) specification of any remaining requirements for funding said loan. This

---

Forms by Exceed 98 Agent Automation (800) 757-3903 www.exceedsystems.com

Initials _____ _____ _____ _____   October 26, 1999 8:22:40 PM Page: 3 of 11
The printed portions of this form, except the *(italicized)* **(differentiated)** insertions, have been approved by the Colorado R
Estate Commission. (CBS 1-9-99)

112

118 condition shall be deemed waived unless Seller receives from Buyer, no later than **Loan Commitment Deadline** (§ 2c),
119 written notice of Buyer's inability to obtain such loan commitment. If Buyer so notifies Seller, this contract shall
120 terminate. **IF BUYER WAIVES THIS CONDITION BUT DOES NOT CLOSE, BUYER SHALL BE IN**
121 **DEFAULT.**
122   **c.**   **Credit Information.** If Buyer is to pay all or part of the Purchase Price by executing a promissory note
123 in favor of Seller or if an existing loan is not to be released at Closing, this contract is conditional upon Seller's approval of
124 Buyer's financial ability and creditworthiness, which approval shall be at Seller's sole and absolute discretion. In such
125 case: (l) Buyer shall supply to Seller by **Buyer's Credit Information Deadline** (§ 2c), at Buyer's expense, information
126 and documents concerning Buyer's financial, employment and credit condition; (2) Buyer consents that Seller may verify
127 Buyer's financial ability and creditworthiness (including obtaining a current credit report); (3) any such information and
128 documents received by Seller shall be held by Seller in confidence, and not released to others except to protect Seller's
129 interest in this transaction; (4) if Seller does not provide written notice of Seller's disapproval to Buyer by **Disapproval of**
130 **Buyer's Credit Deadline** (§ 2c), then Seller waives this condition. If Seller does provide written notice of disapproval to
131 Buyer on or before said date, this contract shall terminate.
132   **d.**   **Existing Loan Review.** If an existing loan is not to be released at Closing, Seller shall provide copies
133 of the loan documents (including note, deed of trust, and any modifications) to Buyer by **Existing Loan Documents**
134 **Deadline** (§ 2c). This contract is conditional upon Buyer's review and approval of the provisions of such loan documents.
135 If written notice of objection to such loan documents, signed by Buyer, is not received by Seller by the **Objection to**
136 **Existing Loan Deadline** (§ 2c), Buyer accepts the terms and conditions of the documents. If the lender's approval of a
137 transfer of the Property is required, this contract is conditional upon Buyer's obtaining such approval without change in
138 the terms of such loan, except as set forth in § 4c. If lender's approval is not obtained by **Approval of Loan Transfer**
139 **Deadline** (§ 2c), this contract shall terminate on such date. If Seller is to be released from liability under such existing
140 loan or if Seller's VA eligibility is to be reinstated and Buyer does not obtain such compliance as set forth in § 4c, this
141 contract may be terminated at Seller's option.
142 **6.**   **APPRAISAL PROVISIONS.**
143   **a.**   **Appraisal Condition.**
144 ☐   **(1)**   **No Appraisal Condition.** This subsection a. shall not apply.
145 ☐   **(2)**   **FHA.** It is expressly agreed that notwithstanding any other provisions of this contract, the
146 Purchaser (Buyer) shall not be obligated to complete the purchase of the Property described herein or to incur any penalty
147 by forfeiture of earnest money deposits or otherwise unless the Purchaser (Buyer) has been given in accordance with
148 HUD/FHA or VA requirements a written statement by the Federal Housing Commissioner, Veterans Administration, or a
149 Direct Endorsement lender setting forth the appraised value of the Property of not less than $_____. The Purchaser
150 (Buyer) shall have the privilege and option of proceeding with consummation of the contract without regard to the
151 amount of the appraised valuation. The appraised valuation is arrived at to determine the maximum mortgage the
152 Department of Housing and Urban Development would insure. HUD does not warrant the value nor the condition of the
153 Property. The Purchaser (Buyer) should satisfy himself/herself that the price and condition of the Property are acceptable.
154 ☐   **(3)**   **VA.** If Buyer is to pay the Purchase Price by obtaining a new VA-guaranteed loan, it is agreed
155 that, notwithstanding any other provisions of this contract, Buyer shall not incur any penalty by forfeiture of earnest
156 money or otherwise be obligated to complete the purchase of the Property described herein, if the contract Purchase Price
157 or cost exceeds the reasonable value of the Property established by the Veterans Administration. Buyer shall, however,
158 have the privilege and option of proceeding with the consummation of this contract without regard to the amount of the
159 reasonable value established by the Veterans Administration.
160 ☐   **(4)**   **Other.** Buyer shall have the sole option and election to terminate this contract if the Purchase
161 Price exceeds the Property's valuation determined by an appraiser engaged by _____. The contract shall terminate by
162 Buyer giving Seller written notice of termination and either a copy of such appraisal or written notice from lender which
163 confirms the Property's valuation is less than the Purchase Price, received on or before the **Appraisal Deadline** (§ 2c). If
164 Seller does not receive such written notice of termination on or before the **Appraisal Deadline** (§ 2c), Buyer waives any
165 right to terminate under this subsection.
166   **b.**   **Cost of Appraisal.** Cost of any appraisal to be obtained after the date of this contract shall be timely
167 paid by ☐ **Buyer** ☐ **Seller.**
168 **7.**   **EVIDENCE OF TITLE.**

Forms by Exceed 98 Agent Automation (800) 757-3903 www.exceedsystems.com

Initials _____ _____ _____ _____   October 26, 1999 8:22:40 PM Page: 4 of 11
The printed portions of this form, except the (*italicized*) (**differentiated**) insertions, have been approved by the Colorado Real
Estate Commission. (CBS 1-9-99)

113

Appendix B

169   **a.**   **Evidence of Title; Survey**. On or before **Title Deadline** (§ 2c), Seller shall cause to be furnished to
170   Buyer, at Seller's expense, a current commitment for owner's title insurance policy in an amount equal to the Purchase
171   Price or if this box is checked, ☐ **An Abstract** of title certified to a current date. If a title insurance commitment is
172   furnished, it ☐ **Shall**   ☐ **Shall Not** commit to delete or insure over the standard exceptions which relate to:

          (1) parties in possession,
          (2) unrecorded easements,
          (3) survey matters,
          (4) any unrecorded mechanics' liens,
          (5) gap period (effective date of commitment to date deed is recorded), and
          (6) unpaid taxes, assessments and unredeemed tax sales prior to the year of Closing.

179   Any additional premium expense to obtain this additional coverage shall be paid by Seller. An amount not to
180   exceed $_____ for the cost of any improvement location certificate or survey shall be paid by ☐ **Buyer**   ☐ **Seller.** If
181   the cost exceeds this amount, Buyer shall pay the excess on or before Closing unless Buyer delivers to Seller or Listing
182   Company, before the improvement location certificate or survey is ordered, Buyer's written notice allowing the exception
183   for survey matters. The improvement location certificate or survey shall be received by Buyer on or before **Survey**
184   **Deadline** (§ 2c). Seller shall cause the title insurance policy to be delivered to Buyer as soon as practicable at or after
185   Closing.

186   **b.**   **Copies of Exceptions**. On or before **Title Deadline** (§ 2c), Seller, at Seller's expense, shall furnish to
187   Buyer, (1) a copy of any plats, declarations, covenants, conditions and restrictions burdening the Property, and (2) if a
188   title insurance commitment is required to be furnished, and if this box is checked ☐ **Copies of any Other Documents**
189   (or, if illegible, summaries of such documents) listed in the schedule of exceptions (Exceptions). Even if the box is not
190   checked, Seller shall have the obligation to furnish these documents pursuant to this subsection if requested by Buyer any
191   time on or before the **Document Request Deadline** (§ 2c). This requirement shall pertain only to documents as shown of
192   record in the office of the clerk and recorder(s). The abstract or title insurance commitment, together with any copies or
193   summaries of such documents furnished pursuant to this Section, constitute the title documents (Title Documents).

195   **c.**   **Common Interest Community Governing Documents.**

197   ☐   **(1) Not Applicable.** This subsection c. shall not apply.
198   ☐   **(2) Conditional on Buyer's Review.** Seller shall cause to be furnished to Buyer, at Seller's expense,
199   on or before **Title Deadline** (§ 2c) a current copy of the owner's association declarations, bylaws, rules and regulations,
200   party wall agreements (herein collectively "Governing Documents"), most recent financial documents consisting of (a)
201   annual balance sheet, (b) annual income and expenditures statement, and (c) annual budget (herein collectively "Financial
202   Documents"), if any. Written notice of any unsatisfactory provision(s) in any of these documents signed by Buyer, or on
203   behalf of Buyer, and given to Seller on or before **Governing Documents Deadline**, [which is the same as **Title**
204   **Objection Deadline** (§ 2c)], shall terminate this contract. If Seller does not receive written notice from Buyer within
205   such time, Buyer accepts the terms of said documents, and Buyer's right to terminate this contract pursuant to this
206   subsection is waived, notwithstanding the provisions of § 8d.
207   ☐   **(3) Not Conditional on Review.** Buyer acknowledges that Seller has delivered a copy of the
208   Governing Documents and Financial Documents. Buyer has reviewed them, agrees to accept the benefits, obligations and
209   restrictions which they impose upon the Property and its owners and waives any right to terminate this contract due to
210   such documents, notwithstanding the provisions of § 8d.
211   **8.**   **TITLE.**
212   **a.**   **Title Review**. Buyer shall have the right to inspect the Title Documents. Written notice by Buyer of
213   unmerchantability of title or of any other unsatisfactory title condition shown by the Title Documents shall be signed by or
214   on behalf of Buyer and given to Seller on or before **Title Objection Deadline** (§ 2c), or within five (5) calendar days after
215   receipt by Buyer of any Title Document(s) or endorsement(s) adding new Exception(s) to the title commitment together
216   with a copy of the Title Document adding new Exception(s) to title. If Seller does not receive Buyer's notice by the
217   date(s) specified above, Buyer accepts the condition of title as disclosed by the Title Documents as satisfactory.
218   **b.**   **Matters not Shown by the Public Records.** Seller shall deliver to Buyer, on or before **Off-Record**
219   **Matters Deadline** (§ 2c) true copies of all lease(s) and survey(s) in Seller's possession pertaining to the Property and shall
220   disclose to Buyer all easements, liens or other title matters not shown by the public records of which Seller has actual

---

Forms by Exceed 98 Agent Automation (800) 757-3903 www.exceedsystems.com

Initials _____ _____ _____ _____   October 26, 1999 8:22:40 PM Page: 5 of 11
The printed portions of this form, except the (*italicized*) (**differentiated**) insertions, have been approved by the Colorado R
Estate Commission. (CBS 1-9-99)

114

221 knowledge. Buyer shall have the right to inspect the Property to determine if any third party(ies) has any right in the
222 Property not shown by the public records (such as an unrecorded easement, unrecorded lease, or boundary line
223 discrepancy). Written notice of any unsatisfactory condition(s) disclosed by Seller or revealed by such inspection shall be
224 signed by or on behalf of Buyer and given to Seller on or before **Off-Record Matters Objection Deadline** (§ 2c). If
225 Seller does not receive Buyer's notice by said date, Buyer accepts title subject to such rights, if any, of third parties of
226 which Buyer has actual knowledge.

227   **c.**   **Special Taxing Districts.** SPECIAL TAXING DISTRICTS MAY BE SUBJECT TO GENERAL OBLIGATION
228 INDEBTEDNESS THAT IS PAID BY REVENUES PRODUCED FROM ANNUAL TAX LEVIES ON THE TAXABLE PROPERTY
229 WITHIN SUCH DISTRICTS. PROPERTY OWNERS IN SUCH DISTRICTS MAY BE PLACED AT RISK FOR INCREASED MILL
230 LEVIES AND EXCESSIVE TAX BURDENS TO SUPPORT THE SERVICING OF SUCH DEBT WHERE CIRCUMSTANCES ARISE
231 RESULTING IN THE INABILITY OF SUCH A DISTRICT TO DISCHARGE SUCH INDEBTEDNESS WITHOUT SUCH AN INCREASE
232 IN MILL LEVIES. BUYER SHOULD INVESTIGATE THE DEBT FINANCING REQUIREMENTS OF THE AUTHORIZED GENERAL
233 OBLIGATION INDEBTEDNESS OF SUCH DISTRICTS, EXISTING MILL LEVIES OF SUCH DISTRICT SERVICING SUCH
234 INDEBTEDNESS, AND THE POTENTIAL FOR AN INCREASE IN SUCH MILL LEVIES.

235   In the event the Property is located within a special taxing district and Buyer desires to terminate this contract as
236 a result, if written notice is received by Seller on or before **Off-Record Matters Objection Deadline** (§ 2c), this contract
237 shall then terminate. If Seller does not receive Buyer's notice by such date, Buyer accepts the effect of the Property's
238 inclusion in such special taxing district(s) and waives the right to so terminate.

239   **d.**   **Right to Cure.** If Seller receives notice of unmerchantability of title or any other unsatisfactory title
240 condition(s) or commitment terms as provided in § 8 a or b above, Seller shall use reasonable effort to correct said items
241 and bear any nominal expense to correct the same prior to Closing. If such unsatisfactory title condition(s) are not
242 corrected on or before Closing, this contract shall then terminate; provided, however, Buyer may, by written notice
243 received by Seller, on or before Closing, waive objection to such items.

244   **e.**   **Right of First Refusal.** If the Governing Documents require written approval of the sale contemplated
245 by this contract or waiver of any option or right of first refusal by the owners' association or any other owner in the
246 owners' association, Seller shall timely submit this contract and request approval of the sale or waiver of any option or
247 right of first refusal pursuant to such provisions. If no such approval or waiver is obtained on or before **Right Of First**
248 **Refusal Deadline** (§ 2c), this contract shall terminate. Buyer agrees to cooperate with Seller in obtaining the approval
249 and/or waiver if required by the applicable Governing Documents and shall make available such information as the owners'
250 association may reasonably require.

251   **f.**   **Title Advisory.** The Title Documents affect the title, ownership and use of the Property and should be
252 reviewed carefully. Additionally, other matters not reflected in the Title Documents may affect the title, ownership and
253 use of the Property, including without limitation boundary lines and encroachments, area, zoning, unrecorded easements
254 and claims of easements, leases and other unrecorded agreements, and various laws and governmental regulations
255 concerning land use, development and environmental matters. The surface estate may be owned separately from the
256 underlying mineral estate, and transfer of the surface estate does not necessarily include transfer of the mineral rights.
257 Third parties may hold interests in oil, gas, other minerals, geothermal energy or water on or under the Property, which
258 interests may give them rights to enter and use the Property. Such matters may be excluded from the title insurance
259 policy. Buyer is advised to timely consult legal counsel with respect to all such matters as there are strict time limits
260 provided in this contract (e.g., **Title Objection Deadline** [§ 2c] and **Off-Record Matters Objection Deadline** [§ 2c]).

262 **9.**   **LEAD-BASED PAINT.** Unless exempt, if the improvements on the Property include one or more residential
263 dwelling(s) for which a building permit was issued prior to January 1, 1978, this contract shall be void unless a completed
264 Lead-Based Paint Disclosure (Sales) form is signed by Seller and the required real estate licensee(s), which must occur
265 prior to the parties signing this contract.

267 **10.**   **PROPERTY DISCLOSURE AND INSPECTION.** On or before **Seller's Property Disclosure Deadline** (§
268 2c), Seller agrees to provide Buyer with a Seller's Property Disclosure form completed by Seller to the best of Seller's
269 current actual knowledge.

270   **a.**   **Inspection Objection Deadline.** Buyer shall have the right to have inspection(s) of the physical
271 condition of the Property and Inclusions, at Buyer's expense. If the physical condition of the Property or Inclusions is
272 unsatisfactory in Buyer's subjective discretion, Buyer shall, on or before **Inspection Objection Deadline** (§ 2c):

Forms by Exceed 98 Agent Automation (800) 757-3903 www.exceedsystems.com

Initials _____ _____ _____ _____   October 26, 1999 8:22:40 PM Page: 6 of 11
The printed portions of this form, except the (*italicized*) (**differentiated**) insertions, have been approved by the Colorado Real
Estate Commission. (CBS 1-9-99)

115

Appendix B

273   **(1)**   notify Seller in writing that this contract is terminated, or
274   **(2)**   provide Seller with a written description of any unsatisfactory physical condition which Buyer
275 requires Seller to correct (Notice to Correct).
276   If written notice is not received by Seller on or before **Inspection Objection Deadline** (§ 2c), the physical
277 condition of the Property and Inclusions shall be deemed to be satisfactory to Buyer.
278   **b.**   **Resolution Deadline**. If a Notice to Correct is received by Seller and if Buyer and Seller have not
279 agreed in writing to a settlement thereof on or before **Resolution Deadline** (§ 2c), this contract shall terminate one
280 calendar day following the **Resolution Deadline** (§ 2c), unless before such termination Seller receives Buyer's written
281 withdrawal of the Notice to Correct.
282   **c.**   **Damage; Liens; Indemnity**. Buyer is responsible for payment for all inspections, surveys, engineering
283 reports or for any other work performed at Buyer's request and shall pay for any damage which occurs to the Property
284 and Inclusions as a result of such activities. Buyer shall not permit claims or liens of any kind against the Property for
285 inspections, surveys, engineering reports and for any other work performed on the Property at Buyer's request. Buyer
286 agrees to indemnify, protect and hold Seller harmless from and against any liability, damage, cost or expense incurred by
287 Seller in connection with any such inspection, claim, or lien. This indemnity includes Seller's right to recover all costs and
288 expenses incurred by Seller to enforce this subsection, including Seller's reasonable attorney fees. The provisions of this
289 subsection shall survive the termination of this contract.
290 **11.**   **CLOSING.** Delivery of deed(s) from Seller to Buyer shall be at Closing (Closing). Closing shall be on the date
291 specified as the **Closing Date** (§ 2c) or by mutual agreement at an earlier date. The hour and place of Closing shall be as
292 designated by _____.
293 **12.**   **TRANSFER OF TITLE.** Subject to tender or payment at Closing as required herein and compliance by Buyer
294 with the other terms and provisions hereof, Seller shall execute and deliver a good and sufficient _____ deed to Buyer, at
295 Closing, conveying the Property free and clear of all taxes except the general taxes for the year of Closing. Except as
296 provided herein, title shall be conveyed free and clear of all liens, including any governmental liens for special
297 improvements installed as of the date of Buyer's signature hereon, whether assessed or not. Title shall be conveyed
298 subject to:
299   **a.**   those specific Exceptions described by reference to recorded documents as reflected in the Title
300 Documents accepted by Buyer in accordance with § 8a [Title Review],
301   **b.**   distribution utility easements (including cable TV),
302   **c.**   those specifically described rights of third parties not shown by the public records of which Buyer has
303 actual knowledge and which were accepted by Buyer in accordance with § 8b [Matters Not Shown by the Public
304 Records], and
305   **d.**   inclusion of the Property within any special taxing district, and
306   **e.**   the benefits and burdens of any declaration and party wall agreements, if any, and
307   **f.**   other:
308 **13.**   **PAYMENT OF ENCUMBRANCES.** Any encumbrance required to be paid shall be paid at or before Closing
309 from the proceeds of this transaction or from any other source.
310 **14.**   **CLOSING COSTS; DOCUMENTS AND SERVICES**. Buyer and Seller shall pay, in Good Funds, their
311 respective Closing costs and all other items required to be paid at Closing, except as otherwise provided herein. Buyer
312 and Seller shall sign and complete all customary or reasonably required documents at or before Closing. Fees for real
313 estate Closing services shall be paid at Closing by ☐ **One-Half by Buyer and One-Half by Seller** ☐   **Buyer** ☐
314 **Seller** ☐ **Other** _____.
315   Any fees incident to the transfer from Seller to Buyer assessed on or on behalf of the owners' association shall be
316 paid by ☐ **Buyer**   ☐ **Seller.**
317   The local transfer tax of _____% of the Purchase Price shall be paid at Closing by ☐ **Buyer**   ☐ **Seller.** Any
318 sales and use tax that may accrue because of this transaction shall be paid when due by ☐ **Buyer**   ☐ **Seller.**
319 **15.**   **PRORATIONS.** The following shall be prorated to **Closing Date** (§ 2c), except as otherwise provided:
320   **a.**   **Taxes.** Personal property taxes, if any, and general real estate taxes for the year of Closing, based on
321 ☐ **The Taxes for the Calendar Year Immediately Preceding Closing**   ☐ **The Most Recent Mill Levy and Most**
322 **Recent Assessment** ☐ **Other** _____.
323   **b.**   **Rents.** Rents based on ☐ **Rents Actually Received**   ☐ **Accrued.** Security deposits held by Seller
324 shall be credited to Buyer. Seller shall assign all leases to Buyer and Buyer shall assume such leases.

Forms by Exceed 98 Agent Automation (800) 757-3903 www.exceedsystems.com

Initials _____ _____ _____ _____   October 26, 1999 8:22:40 PM Page: 7 of 11
The printed portions of this form, except the (*italicized*) (**differentiated**) insertions, have been approved by the Colorado R
Estate Commission. (CBS 1-9-99)

116

325   c.   **Association Assessments.** Current regular owners' association assessments and association dues.
326 Owners' association assessments paid in advance shall be credited to Seller at Closing. Cash reserves held out of the
327 regular owners' association assessments for deferred maintenance by the owners' association shall not be credited to Seller
328 except as may be otherwise provided by the Governing Documents. Any special assessment by the owners' association for
329 improvements that have been installed as of the date of Buyer's signature hereon shall be the obligation of Seller. Any
330 other special assessment assessed prior to **Closing Date** (§ 2c) by the owners' association shall be the obligation of ☐
331 **Buyer**   ☐ **Seller.** Seller represents that the amount of the regular owners' association assessment is currently payable
332 at $_____ per _____ and that there are no unpaid regular or special assessments against the Property except the current
333 regular assessments and except _____.
334 Such assessments are subject to change as provided in the Governing Documents. Seller agrees to promptly request the
335 owners' association to deliver to Buyer before **Closing Date** (§ 2c) a current statement of assessments against the
336 Property. Any fees incident to the issuance of such statement of assessments shall be paid by ☐ **Buyer**   ☐ **Seller.**
337   d.   **Loan Assumption - Mortgage Insurance.** FHA or private mortgage insurance premium, if any, ☐
338 **Shall**   ☐ **Shall Not** be apportioned to **Closing Date** (§ 2c). Any such amount shall be apportioned as follows:_____.
339   e.   **Other Prorations.** Water, sewer charges; and interest on continuing loan(s), if any; and _____.
340   f.   **Final Settlement.** Unless otherwise agreed in writing, these prorations shall be final.
341 **16.**   **POSSESSION.** Possession of the Property shall be delivered to Buyer on **Possession Date** and **Possession**
342 **Time** (§ 2c), subject to the following lease(s) or tenancy(s):_____.
343   If Seller, after Closing, fails to deliver possession as specified, Seller shall be subject to eviction and shall be
344 additionally liable to Buyer for payment of $_____ per day from the **Possession Date** (§ 2c) until possession is delivered.
345   Buyer ☐ **Does**   ☐ **Does Not** represent that Buyer will occupy the Property as Buyer's principal residence.
346 **17.**   **NOT ASSIGNABLE:** This contract shall not be assignable by Buyer without Seller's prior written consent.
347 Except as so restricted, this contract shall inure to the benefit of and be binding upon the heirs, personal representatives,
348 successors and assigns of the parties.
349 **18.**   **CONDITION OF, AND DAMAGE TO PROPERTY AND INCLUSIONS.** Except as otherwise provided in
350 this contract, the Property, Inclusions or both shall be delivered in the condition existing as of the date of this contract,
351 ordinary wear and tear excepted.
352   a.   **Casualty; Insurance.** In the event the Property or Inclusions shall be damaged by fire or other casualty
353 prior to Closing, in an amount of not more than ten percent of the total Purchase Price, Seller shall be obligated to repair
354 the same before the **Closing Date** (§ 2c). In the event such damage is not repaired within said time or if the damages
355 exceed such sum, this contract may be terminated at the option of Buyer by delivering to Seller written notice of
356 termination. Should Buyer elect to carry out this contract despite such damage, Buyer shall be entitled to a credit, at
357 Closing, for all the insurance proceeds resulting from such damage to the Property and Inclusions payable to Seller but not
358 the owners' association, if any, plus the amount of any deductible provided for in such insurance policy, such credit not to
359 exceed the total Purchase Price.
360   b.   **Damage; Inclusions; Services.** Should any Inclusion(s) or service(s) (including systems and
361 components of the Property, e.g. heating, plumbing, etc.) fail or be damaged between the date of this contract and Closing
362 or possession, whichever shall be earlier, then Seller shall be liable for the repair or replacement of such Inclusion(s) or
363 service(s) with a unit of similar size, age and quality, or an equivalent credit, but only to the extent that the maintenance or
364 replacement of such Inclusion(s), service(s) or fixture(s) is not the responsibility of the owners' association, if any, less any
365 insurance proceeds received by Buyer covering such repair or replacement. Seller and Buyer are aware of the existence of
366 pre-owned home warranty programs which may be purchased and may cover the repair or replacement of some
367 Inclusion(s).
368   c.   **Walk-Through; Verification of Condition.** Buyer, upon reasonable notice, shall have the right to
369 walk through the Property prior to Closing to verify that the physical condition of the Property and Inclusions complies
370 with this contract.
371 **19.**   **RECOMMENDATION OF LEGAL AND TAX COUNSEL.** By signing this document, Buyer and Seller
372 acknowledge that the Selling Company or the Listing Company has advised that this document has important legal
373 consequences and has recommended the examination of title and consultation with legal and tax or other counsel before
374 signing this contract.

Forms by Exceed 98 Agent Automation (800) 757-3903   www.exceedsystems.com

Initials _____   _____   _____   _____   October 26, 1999 8:22:40 PM Page: 8 of 11
The printed portions of this form, except the (*italicized*) (**differentiated**) insertions, have been approved by the Colorado Real
Estate Commission. (CBS 1-9-99)

117

375   **20.**   **TIME OF ESSENCE AND REMEDIES.** Time is of the essence hereof. If any note or check received as
376   Earnest Money hereunder or any other payment due hereunder is not paid, honored or tendered when due, or if any other
377   obligation hereunder is not performed or waived as herein provided, there shall be the following remedies:

378   **a.**   **If Buyer is in Default**:

379   ☐   **(1)**   **Specific Performance.** Seller may elect to treat this contract as canceled, in which case all
380   payments and things of value received hereunder shall be forfeited and retained on behalf of Seller, and Seller may recover
381   such damages as may be proper, or Seller may elect to treat this contract as being in full force and effect and Seller shall
382   have the right to specific performance or damages, or both.

383   ☐   **(2)**   **Liquidated Damages.** All payments and things of value received hereunder shall be forfeited
384   by Buyer and retained on behalf of Seller and both parties shall thereafter be released from all obligations hereunder. It is
385   agreed that such payments and things of value are LIQUIDATED DAMAGES and (except as provided in subsection c)
386   are SELLER'S SOLE AND ONLY REMEDY for Buyer's failure to perform the obligations of this contract. Seller
387   expressly waives the remedies of specific performance and additional damages.

388   **b.**   **If Seller is in Default**: Buyer may elect to treat this contract as canceled, in which case all payments
389   and things of value received hereunder shall be returned and Buyer may recover such damages as may be proper, or Buyer
390   may elect to treat this contract as being in full force and effect and Buyer shall have the right to specific performance or
391   damages, or both.

392   **c.**   **Costs and Expenses**. In the event of any arbitration or litigation relating to this contract, the arbitrator
393   or court shall award to the prevailing party all reasonable costs and expenses, including attorney fees.

394   **21.**   **MEDIATION.** If a dispute arises relating to this contract, prior to or after Closing, and is not resolved, the
395   parties shall first proceed in good faith to submit the matter to mediation. Mediation is a process in which the parties
396   meet with an impartial person who helps to resolve the dispute informally and confidentially. Mediators cannot impose
397   binding decisions. The parties to the dispute must agree before any settlement is binding. The parties will jointly appoint
398   an acceptable mediator and will share equally in the cost of such mediation. The mediation, unless otherwise agreed, shall
399   terminate in the event the entire dispute is not resolved 30 calendar days from the date written notice requesting mediation
400   is sent by one party to the other(s). This Section shall not alter any date in this contract, unless otherwise agreed.

401   **22.**   **EARNEST MONEY DISPUTE.** Notwithstanding any termination of this contract, Buyer and Seller agree that,
402   in the event of any controversy regarding the Earnest Money and things of value held by broker or Closing Company
403   (unless mutual written instructions are received by the holder of the Earnest Money and things of value), broker or
404   Closing Company shall not be required to take any action but may await any proceeding, or at broker's or Closing
405   Company's option and sole discretion, may interplead all parties and deposit any moneys or things of value into a court of
406   competent jurisdiction and shall recover court costs and reasonable attorney fees.

407   **23.**   **TERMINATION.** In the event this contract is terminated, all payments and things of value received hereunder
408   shall be returned and the parties shall be relieved of all obligations hereunder, subject to §§ 10c, 21 and 22.

409   **24.**   **ADDITIONAL PROVISIONS**. (The language of these additional provisions has not been approved by the
410   Colorado Real Estate Commission.)

411
412
413

414   **25.**   **ENTIRE AGREEMENT; SUBSEQUENT MODIFICATION; SURVIVAL**. This contract constitutes the
415   entire contract between the parties relating to the subject hereof, and any prior agreements pertaining thereto, whether
416   oral or written, have been merged and integrated into this contract. No subsequent modification of any of the terms of this
417   contract shall be valid, binding upon the parties, or enforceable unless made in writing and signed by the parties. Any
418   obligation in this contract which, by its terms, is intended to be performed after termination or Closing shall survive the
419   same.

420   **26.**   **FACSIMILE.** Signatures ☐ **May**   ☐ **May Not** be evidenced by facsimile. Documents with original
421   signatures shall be provided to the other party at Closing, or earlier upon request of any party.

422   **27.**   **NOTICE.** Except for the notice requesting mediation described in § 21, any notice to Buyer shall be effective
423   when received by Buyer or by Selling Company and any notice to Seller shall be effective when received by Seller or
424   Listing Company.

425   **28.**   **NOTICE OF ACCEPTANCE; COUNTERPARTS**. This proposal shall expire unless accepted in writing, by
426   Buyer and Seller, as evidenced by their signatures below, and the offering party receives notice of acceptance pursuant to

---

Forms by Exceed 98 Agent Automation (800) 757-3903 www.exceedsystems.com

Initials _____ _____ _____ _____   October 26, 1999 8:22:40 PM Page: 9 of 11
The printed portions of this form, except the **(*italicized*) (differentiated)** insertions, have been approved by the Colorado R
Estate Commission. (CBS 1-9-99)

118

427 § 27 on or before **Acceptance Deadline Date** and **Acceptance Deadline Time** (§ 2c). If accepted, this document shall
428 become a contract between Seller and Buyer. A copy of this document may be executed by each party, separately, and
429 when each party has executed a copy thereof, such copies taken together shall be deemed to be a full and complete
430 contract between the parties.
431
432
433

_____   _____
                                                  Buyer
Date of Buyer's signature   Date of Buyer's signature
Buyer's Address:
Buyer's Telephone No: Buyer's Fax No:

[NOTE: If this offer is being countered or rejected, do not sign this document. Refer to § 29

_____   _____
Seller   Seller

Date of Seller's signature   Date of Seller's signature

Seller's Address
Seller's Telephone No: Seller's Fax No:

434
435 **29.   COUNTER; REJECTION.** This offer is ☐ **Countered**   ☐ **Rejected**.
436 **Initials only of party (Buyer or Seller) who countered or rejected offer** _____
437
438   **END OF CONTRACT**
439 | Note: Closing Instructions should be signed on or before Title Deadline. |
440
441
442 **BROKER ACKNOWLEDGMENTS.** The undersigned Broker(s) acknowledges receipt of the Earnest Money deposit
443 specified in § 4 and, while not a party to the contract, agrees to cooperate upon request with any mediation conducted
444 under
445 § 21.
446   **Selling Company Brokerage Relationship**. The Selling Company and its licensees have been engaged in this
447 transaction as ☐ **Buyer Agent**   ☐ **Seller Agent/Subagent**   ☐ **Dual Agent**   ☐ **Transaction-Broker**.
448   **Listing Company Brokerage Relationship**. The Listing Company and its licensees have been engaged in this
449 transaction as ☐ **Seller Agent**   ☐ **Dual Agent**   ☐ **Transaction-Broker**.
450
451 **BROKERS' COMPENSATION DISCLOSURE.**
452 Selling Company's compensation or commission is to be paid by:
453 ☐ **Buyer**   ☐ **Seller**   ☐ **Listing Company**   ☐ **Other** _____.
454 (To be completed by Listing Company) Listing Company's compensation or commission is to be paid by:
455 ☐ **Buyer**   ☐ **Seller**   ☐ **Other**
456
457
458 Selling Company: RE/MAX Properties of the Summit (Name of Company)
459
460 By: _____
461 Signature Ken Deshaies Broker Associate   Date
462 Selling Company 's Address: 131 Blue River Parkway, Silverthorne P.O. Drawer 2929, Dillon, CO 80435
463 Selling Company 's Telephone No 468-2000 Selling Company 's Fax No:
464

Initials _____ _____   October 26, 1999 8:22:40 PM

Appendix B

465   Listing Company: _____ (Name of Company)
466
467   By: _____
468   Signature   Date
469   Listing Company 's Address:
470   Listing Company 's Telephone No: _____   Listing Company 's Fax No:

APPENDIX C

Sample Clauses for The Contract to Buy and Sell Real Estate

(Note: Language in these clauses has not been approved by the Colorado Real Estate Commission. They are provided as examples only and are meant to bring to your attention issues which you might want to address in your offer to purchase. Your Realtor® may use similar or dissimilar language to accomplish the same result. Consult with your Realtor® or your attorney on the use of any language in your contract.)

Sample Clauses

(Note that the use of an asterisk (*) in any clause below indicates the need for information. You and your Realtor® should determine the information—number or data—needed in each instance. Of course, you should also discuss the applicability of any of the following, or other, clauses before finalizing an offer.)

Buyer's Right to Change Financing.

Buyer reserves the right to change loan programs as long as the net proceeds to Seller under this contract remain the same.

Working Order.

Seller represents that all of the appliances, systems, and utilities servicing the Property will be in working order at the time of delivery of possession to Buyer.

Automatic Extension.

In the event Buyer's loan has not been approved by the deadline set in Section 2c due to delays in loan processing caused by parties other than the Buyer, then loan approval, closing and possession deadlines shall automatically be extended for up to * calendar days.

Carpet Cleaning.

Seller will have the carpets professionally steam cleaned within 48 hours prior to closing if the Property is occupied, or anytime prior to closing if the Property is and will remain unoccupied until closing.

There are times when, for convenience or expedience, you may make an offer individually, fully intending to take title in the name of a company or to add a spouse or other partners. If so, consider the following:

Assignability of Contract.

Notwithstanding the provisions of Section 17 herein, Seller acknowledges that Buyer intends to form a company prior to closing in which name Buyer intends to take title. This will not release Buyer of the obligation to provide financial information to Seller, and Buyer agrees to sign individually on any loan herein.

—or—

Notwithstanding the provisions of Section 17 herein, Seller acknowledges that Buyer intends to add one or more partners to this contract prior to closing, and that title will be taken in the name(s) of all partners. This will not release Buyer of the obligation to provide financial information to Seller, and Buyer agrees that Buyer and additional partners will each sign on any loan herein.

When you are selling an investment property and replacing it by purchasing another through a 1031 exchange, consider the following:

Section 1031 Exchange.

Seller shall cooperate in structuring this transaction as a like-kind exchange for the benefit of Buyer, as long as Seller incurs no additional cost. Despite the anti-assignment provision of Section 17 herein, Buyer has the right to assign its rights and obligations under this contract to an entity acting as Qualified Intermediary (as defined in Internal Revenue Code Section 1031) to complete the like-kind exchange; but assignment shall not release Buyer from liability for performance of any of its obligations. In the interest of convenience, however, Seller shall convey title to the Property and Inclusions directly to Buyer on behalf of the Qualified Intermediary. This subsection is not intended to waive any of the deadlines or other obligations of Buyer in this contract. Buyer acknowledges being advised to seek the guidance of tax counsel in completing this Section 1031 Exchange.

When you have to sell one property in order to purchase another, it is incumbent on you to solicit the Seller's cooperation, both for the sale and, ideally, for the coordination of closing dates. The following two clauses may help:

Sale of Buyer's Other Property.

Buyer shall have the right to terminate this contract at any time prior to * if Buyer has not sold certain "Other Property" owned by Buyer and described as *, on terms acceptable to Buyer. If Buyer has not given Seller written notice of said termination by the deadline in this subsection, Buyer shall be deemed to have waived this contingency. If Buyer does not sell the other Property by the deadline and does not terminate this contract as provided in this subsection, and if this contract then fails to close because Buyer fails to qualify for any financing described in Section 4b, Buyer shall forfeit to Seller all earnest money deposited hereunder. If Buyer does not have the Other Property under contract and does not provide Seller with a copy of the executed contract by *, Seller shall have the right to terminate this contract by giving written notice to Buyer within five days thereafter. Seller may continue to market the Property. If, prior to the deadline in this subsection, Seller receives an acceptable bona fide offer from a third party to purchase the Property, Buyer shall have three calendar days following notice thereof in which to either waive this contingency or to terminate this contract. Failure by Buyer to elect one of these two options shall be deemed a waiver of this contingency.

Change and Coordination Of Closing.

Seller hereby agrees to change the closing date herein and coordinate same with the closing of Buyer's Other Property, should a contract to purchase the Other Property designate a closing date other than that set herein. Buyer agrees to make a good faith effort to negotiate a closing date on said purchase contract to match the closing date herein. In Buyer is unable to do so, however, Seller agrees to extend the closing herein by up to * days if necessary to make such closings happen on the same day.